Financial and Monetary Policy Studies

Volume 56

The book series 'Financial and Monetary Policy Studies' features the latest research in financial and monetary economics. Books published in this series are primarily monographs and edited volumes that present new research results, both theoretical and empirical, on a clearly defined topic. All books are published in print and digital formats and disseminated globally.

Lucia Milena Murgia

The Impact of Monetary Policy

Estimation Methodologies and Empirical Evidence

Springer

Lucia Milena Murgia
School of Management
University College London
London, UK

ISSN 0921-8580 ISSN 2197-1889 (electronic)
Financial and Monetary Policy Studies
ISBN 978-3-032-15450-7 ISBN 978-3-032-15451-4 (eBook)
https://doi.org/10.1007/978-3-032-15451-4

This Springer imprint is published by the registered company Springer Nature Switzerland AG
The registered company address is: Gewerbestrasse 11, 6330 Cham, Switzerland

Acknowledgements

Writing this book has been an intellectually enriching and personally transformative journey. It is a work that stands on the shoulders of many individuals and institutions whose support, guidance, and encouragement have been indispensable. I am deeply indebted to all those who have, in various ways, contributed to the completion of this project.

First and foremost, I extend my sincere gratitude to my supervisors at Norwich Business School, whose intellectual mentorship and constructive criticism have been invaluable throughout my academic journey. Their insightful guidance helped refine my thinking, sharpen my analytical framework, and strengthen the rigor of my arguments. They challenged me to question assumptions, explore alternative perspectives, and remain committed to academic integrity. Their encouragement and trust in my abilities were constant sources of motivation.

I am equally grateful to my colleagues in the Finance Group at Norwich Business School. Working alongside such a talented and collaborative community has been both a privilege and an inspiration. The stimulating conversations in seminars, the informal debates over coffee, and the generous exchange of ideas have enriched my understanding of finance, economics, and the nuanced interplay between monetary policy and real-world markets. The collegial spirit within our group not only made my research better but also made the process far more enjoyable.

I would also like to acknowledge the broader academic community that has shaped my thinking. The conferences, workshops, and seminars I attended during my doctoral and postdoctoral years provided valuable opportunities to present my ideas, receive constructive feedback, and engage with scholars whose work has influenced my own. These interactions reinforced my belief that the study of monetary policy is as much a collaborative endeavour as it is an individual one.

On a personal note, I am profoundly thankful to my family and friends for their unwavering support. Their patience, understanding, and encouragement sustained me through the long hours of research and writing. They provided the balance and perspective needed to persevere through challenges and celebrate small victories along the way.

I also hope that this book will be of practical value to future PhD students who aspire to enter the field of monetary policy research. Many of the applied insights and methodological considerations presented here would have been invaluable to me during my own doctoral journey. If this work can help guide others through the complexities of designing, executing, and communicating rigorous research, it will have fulfilled an important purpose beyond its academic contribution.

Finally, this book is dedicated to all those who believe in the power of rigorous economic analysis to inform better policy decisions. Monetary policy has far-reaching implications for economies and societies, and it is my hope that the insights contained in these pages will contribute, even in a modest way, to the on-going dialogue between scholars, policymakers, and the public.

To everyone who has been part of this journey, whether through direct academic collaboration, institutional support, or personal encouragement, please accept my deepest thanks. This work is as much yours as it is mine.

Contents

1 **Introduction** 1
Reference 4

2 **The Responses of Monetary Policy to Macroeconomic Cycles** 5
2.1 Introduction 5
2.2 Inflation Pressures and Monetary Policy: From the Great Inflation to Systemic Reform 9
2.3 From the Great Inflation to the 2008 Financial Crisis 12
2.4 The Response to the Crisis 14
2.5 Exogenous Shocks 16
2.5.1 A Political Shock: Brexit 17
2.5.2 A Completely Unforeseen Scenario: COVID-19 18
2.5.3 Post COVID-19 Economy 19
References 21

3 **The Disclosure of Monetary Policy to the Public** 23
3.1 Introduction 23
3.2 The Evolution of Central Banks Communication Policies 24
3.2.1 The Federal Reserve and Its Chairs 24
3.2.2 The European Central Bank and Its Presidents 30
3.2.3 Bank of England and Its Governors 32
3.3 New Developments of the Communication Strategy 33
References 34

4 **The Effects of the Disclosure to Financial Markets: Monetary Policy Announcements, Surprises, and Asset Pricing** 37
4.1 Introduction 37
4.2 Monetary Policy Surprises and Asset Pricing 38
4.2.1 Industry Measures Employing Federal Funds Futures 41
4.3 Macroeconomic Announcements and Asset Pricing 43
4.3.1 The FOMC Puzzle 44

4.3.2 The FOMC Puzzle and International Evidence 48
4.3.3 Macroeconomic Attention 49
References 50

5 How Do We Measure the Economic Impact of Monetary Policy? ... 53
5.1 Introduction 53
5.2 Assessing the Impact of Monetary Policy Shocks: Early Vector Autoregressive Approaches 56
5.3 The Narrative Approach 59
5.3.1 Applications of the Narrative Identification Strategy 62
5.4 Sign-Restrictions 64
5.5 A Review of the Advent of High-Frequency Data 65
5.6 Estimation via Local Projections 70
References 72

6 Estimating Monetary Policy Shocks: Data and Practical Aspects ... 75
6.1 Introduction 75
6.2 R Packages and Examples of Implementation 76
6.2.1 Developing a Narrative Shock Series for Europe 77
6.2.2 The Shock Series Effects on Macroeconomic Variables ... 83
6.2.3 High-Frequency Evidence 90
6.3 Available Datasets and Replication Files 94
References 94

List of Abbreviations

APP	Asset Purchase Programme
AR	Autoregressive
BOE	Bank of England
BOJ	Bank of Japan
BPS	Basis Points
BTC	Bitcoin
CBPP	Covered Bond Purchase Programme
CDOs	Collateralized Debt Obligations
CDS	Credit Default Swaps
CME	Chicago Mercantile Exchange
CME Group	Chicago Mercantile Exchange Group (CME, CBOT, NYMEX, COMEX)
CPI	Consumer Price Index
CSPP	Corporate Sector Purchase Programme
DE	Digital Euro
ECB	European Central Bank
EFFR	Effective Federal Funds Rate
ETH	Ethereum
FCA	Financial Conduct Authority
FED	Federal Reserve
FOMC	Federal Open Market Committee
GDP	Gross Domestic Product
GSEs	Government-Sponsored Enterprises
HF	High-Frequency
HICP	Harmonized Index of Consumer Prices
IFB	Inflation-Forecast-Based
IR	Inflation Report
IRF	Impulse Response Function
IT	Inflation Targeting
LIBOR	London Interbank Offered Rate
LP	Local Projections

LTRO	Longer-Term Refinancing Operations
MAI	Macroeconomic Attention Index
MBS	Mortgage-Backed Securities
MPC	Monetary Policy Committee
MPI	Monetary Policy Innovation
MPS	Monetary Policy Shock
MRO	Main Refinancing Operations
NBER	National Bureau of Economic Research
PPI	Producer Price Index
PEPP	Pandemic Emergency Purchase Programme
PSPP	Public Sector Purchase Programme
QPM	Quarterly Projection Model
QE	Quantitative Easing
R&R	Romer & Romer
S&P 500	Standard & Poor's 500 (index)
SEP	Summary of Economic Projections
SMP	Securities Markets Programme
SPF	Survey of Professional Forecasters
SVAR	Structural Vector Autoregressive
SVI	Google Search Volume Index
TARP	Troubled Asset Relief Program
TIBOR	Tokyo Interbank Offered Rate
US	United States
VAR	Vector Autoregressive
VIX	Volatility Index
ZLB	Zero-Lower Bound

List of Figures

Fig. 2.1 CPI for the United States. The figure presents the level of inflation as the yearly variation of the Consumer Price Index the United States. Source: World Bank via FRED 7
Fig. 2.2 Federal funds rate. The graph presents the level of the Federal Funds Target rate from the 01/1960 until 04/2025. Source: FRED . . . 13
Fig. 2.3 The UK market 22/06/2016–15/08/2016. The graph plots the daily Bank Rate, and the daily FTSE 100 index, between 22/06/2016 and 15/08/2016. Source: Bank of England, Investing 17
Fig. 5.1 Interest rate path. The figure plots the reference interest for the United Kingdom (Bank Rate - UK) and for the United States (Federal Funds Target rate—US) from January 1997 until July 2023. Source: FRED and Bank of England 55
Fig. 6.1 R console. The figure shows an example of a dataset shown in the R console. Source: Author's Computation 79
Fig. 6.2 Exogenous monetary shocks—ECB. The figure presents the shock series computed extracting the residuals from Eq. (6.1). Along with the shock series we plot the series of the target interest rate. Source: Author's Computations 83
Fig. 6.3 Full local projections output. The figure includes the full output of model 6.2 for all the variables. The first row includes the effect of inflation on all the other variables. The second row includes the effect of unemployment on all the other variables. The third row includes the effect of the commodity index on all the variables. Lastly, the fourth line includes the effect of our measure of shocks on all the other variables. Source: Authors Computations 85
Fig. 6.4 Local projection output for prices and output. The figure presents an extraction of Fig. 6.3, where only the effects of "SHOCKS" on Inflation and unemployment are considered. Source: Author's Computations 89

Fig. 6.5 MK series analysis. The figure represents an extraction of the output of model 6.2, when the shock series is represented by the series of Kerssenfischer (2022). The effect of the HF shock series is shown on stocks, inflation, unemployment and a Eurozone Investment Grade Bond index. Source: Author's Computations . . . 90

List of Tables

Table 2.1 Pros and cons of inflation targeting framework. 11
Table 2.2 Average CPI United States 12
Table 3.1 Documents published by the FED. 26
Table 4.1 Post-pandemic data 39
Table 6.1 Variables in Eq. (6.1). 77
Table 6.2 First stage VAR 80
Table 6.3 Monetary policy shocks and their effect on output and prices 91

Chapter 1
Introduction

Central Banks around the world make conventional and unconventional monetary policy decisions as changes occur in the macroeconomic cycle. For example, they may undertake conventional (also known as "plain-vanilla") decisions when maintaining "price stability" by adjusting the short-term reference interest rate to counter inflation risks. These decisions, however, typically become less important when reference interest rates inch closer to the inflation target. Central Banks may also intervene to stimulate the macroeconomy by injecting liquidity into the banking system or buying significant amounts of assets in financial markets. These direct interventions of central banks in financial markets impose demand pressures on selected assets, raise their prices but lower their yields. They are known as "quantitative easing" policies. These actions have had greater importance in the year 2008, when they were first experimented with the disruptive effects of the great crisis that erupted in the US financial markets. Those policies have later been adopted by other central banks. Notably, the European central bank adopted these actions to confront the severe sovereign debt crisis of 2011–2012. They have also been an important means of intervention of major central banks during the recent Covid-19 pandemic crisis in 2020.

Economists and financial experts have long been debating how monetary policy works. The crucial question in the debate has been "what is the economic impact of monetary policy decisions?". Assessing the economic impact of monetary policy surprises or shocks is crucial for understanding the validity of policy transmission channels. Among economists, it is also important to distinguish which policy decisions better fit with proposed macroeconomic models. As of today, an extensive body of research has concluded that central bank policies have a significant impact on the real economy, mostly through the important channel of financial markets. An accepted interpretation of the extant literature is that monetary policy decisions are driven by financial conditions and have significant financial market effects such as exerting their influence on asset prices and risk premiums. For example, easing monetary policy brings down risk premiums in stock, treasuries, corporate bonds,

L. M. Murgia, *The Impact of Monetary Policy*, Financial and Monetary Policy Studies 56, https://doi.org/10.1007/978-3-032-15451-4_1

and foreign exchange markets. At the same time, reducing interest rates could make easier credit conditions, and so it could affect bank lending. One consequence will be that banks could accept lower interest rate spreads to grant loans to the corporate and household sectors.

This book is intended to be useful to students, economists, and central bankers who may find in it direct and compact readings of specialized topics related to the economic impact of central banks' decisions in financial markets. The book has been designed to first introduce a review of the "state of the art" of this area of research, with a focus on the economic impact of monetary policy shocks. Next, it will move forward by providing some fresh perspectives and novel empirical evidence that takes stock of more recent econometric methods that wish to address concerns and critiques in how to identify the causal effects of monetary policy innovations.

To achieve these ambitious goals, I build up the reader's background with a summary of the vast and complex research area that has been tackling those questions. I specifically explore how and when this line of research started, how it developed in its methods and types of used data, and what is now the consensus on the impact of monetary policy decisions on the economic system.

This book is structured through its chapters as follows:

- Chapter 2 reviews how central banks have been confronting macroeconomic cycles. Initially, I point specifically to the area of research that examines the impact of monetary policies that target inflation and, in some cases, full employment. Monetary policy interventions are discussed in each historical context to provide a comprehensive and coherent view of both the macroeconomic cycles, policies, and countries that have evolved in the last decades.
- Chapter 3 introduces the reader to the literature on communication policies of central banks. The literature of central bank disclosures has been intensively evolving in the last decade. That area of research has been paralleling and following the central bank use of new communication tools and technologies and their carefully selected announcement timing. Now, the consensus of extant research is that when central bankers talk, financial markets listen—intently (Blinder et al., 2022). That consensus highlights an important characteristic of the typical communication policy of a central bank: disclosures are normally expected to reach out to financial markets experts. In more recent times, central banks are contemplating to extending their disclosure talks and statements to a larger audience, being able to reach and be clearly understood by the general public. Central bank communication has been transforming because of the significant impact that their statements and messages have on the economic system. Literature has found that those communications affect financial markets prices and risk premiums, bank lending policies, enterprises, and consumers' investment and financing decisions. All in all, when central banks talk, we should expect important changes that spill over to financial markets and to the real economy.

- Chapter 4 is designed to further expand the reader's knowledge and understanding of central bank disclosure policies. Its focus is on monetary shocks and surprises, their unintended effects, and how financial markets typically react to unexpected central bank communications. The chapter introduces the reader to the so-called puzzles of the monetary announcement literature. The puzzle refers to financial market behaviour "prior" to the FOMC (Federal Open Market Committee) announcement. The financial market anticipated reaction extends to several assets and risk premiums. The literature examines the role of asset pricing theory in explaining the effects on international financial market prices and risk premiums. One of the novel results of that literature is the highly significant relation between theoretical risk premiums and monetary policy surprise. A relation that a large body of research does not find in non-announcement periods.
- Chapter 5 analyses the statistical and econometric methods that researchers have been using to estimate the economic impact of monetary policy. The chapter delves into the methodological developments of the last decades that have been adopted by researchers to investigate the key question. At the same time, an intense debate has evolved to address the many concerns that the literature has raised on the appropriateness of each proposed method. The reader will be first presented with early vector autoregressive technique. That method has been the literature's pillar since Sims (1980)s milestone article. Subsequently, new methods based on the use of external instruments have been gradually taking a prominent role in that literature. A crucial moment in that literature's development has been the financial crisis of 2008 in the US and the subsequent contagion to the world economy. Monetary policy actions and techniques had to adapt hastily to the new economic environment. New concepts in monetary policy discussion emerged, such as examining systemic effects and affirming the important goal of financial stability. The chapter is also presenting how new data types—such as high frequency—have been earning an important place in studies that analyse the economic impact of monetary policy surprises. That type of data mostly is sourced from derivatives markets, where the quality of price adjustment and speed of price discovery are now considered better than in main spot markets.
- Chapter 6 is intended to guide the reader, particularly young scholars, in the complex array of steps and procedures to replicate the most relevant papers I review in the book. The chapter provides examples to make easier the reproduction of selected seminal papers.

To this end, I supply a comprehensive list of references that focus on the key research question that is the ultimate goal of this book. Thus, the examples of replication steps should be able to conduct the research to obtain those results and with a different dataset to observe differences and increase the literature's understanding.

Reference

Blinder, A. S., Ehrmann, M., de Haan, J., & Jansen, D.-J. (2022). *Central Bank communication with the general public: Promise or false hope?* NBER # 30277.

Sims, C. A. (1980). Macroeconomics and reality. *Econometrica, 48*(1), 1–48.

Chapter 2
The Responses of Monetary Policy to Macroeconomic Cycles

2.1 Introduction

> The principal policy tool for maintaining macroeconomic stability is monetary policy. In normal times, the Fed and other central banks use open market operations—purchases and sales of securities in markets—to move interest rates up or down, and in doing so try to create a more stable macroeconomic environment
>
> Ben S. Bernanke, "Lecture 2: The Federal Reserve after World War II in The Federal Reserve and the Financial Crisis (2012)".

Monetary Policy is the set of tools, by which a central bank attempts to influence the cost and supply of money. As highlighted in the definition given by Ben Bernanke, the goal is a stable macroeconomic environment. A stable macroeconomic environment, which across the years has become the Inflation Targeting (IT) framework. A stable economic environment needs stable prices. To do so, central banks have gradually expanded their set of tools and moved from the setting of interest rates to the influence of liquidity facilities, forward guidance, balance-sheet operations, and, in extreme circumstances, direct asset purchases.

Despite this growing toolbox, the underlying objectives have remained remarkably consistent: achieve and maintain price stability, support sustainable employment, economic growth, and safeguard the financial system against destabilizing shocks. Although different central banks have identified different mandates, the endogenous relationship of macroeconomic variables blends it into one constantly evolving process and of setting monetary policy, assessing it, evaluating it, correcting it, with often many difficulties in disentangling the effects (more on this in Chap. 5).

The story begins after the World Conflict era, when many advanced economies operated under fixed-exchange-rate regimes, policymakers lending to governments was commonplace, and policy frameworks often leaned heavily on monetary aggregates or exchange-rate pegs. In the early 1970s, the Bretton Woods system collapsed, when the persistent US deficits in the balance of payments led to the US

L. M. Murgia, *The Impact of Monetary Policy*, Financial and Monetary Policy Studies 56, https://doi.org/10.1007/978-3-032-15451-4_2

gold stock to be lower than the value of US dollars held by foreigners. Further, and along with flower power came two oil-price shocks (1973 and 1979), which led to a period also known as "stagflation". The latter term refers to a period where most advanced economics, and mostly the US, experienced extremely high inflation, economic stagnation, and rising unemployment. The term "Stagflation" has been repeatedly used across the years to describe a similar macroeconomic environment. The very recent tariff policies brought forward by the US President Donald Trump heightened the risk of stagflation, as commented by the Federal Reserve.[1]

During the stagflation period, central banks were lacking clear mandates, and their communication tools were very limited, if not totally absent. Policymakers were fighting the conundrum between controlling inflation and unemployment, with a series of tightening and easing. This *modus operandi* produced a very volatile economic environment and undermined public confidence. In August 1979, Paul Volcker shifted the target from the interest rate to monetary aggregates and allowed short-term interest rates to climb up to 20% in 1981.[2]

Figure 2.1 shows the sharp decline in Inflation after 1980. Inflation fell and the Federal Reserve's credibility was restored. The recession was deep, even though for a relatively short period of time. The interventions that preceded the fall of inflation, however, seem short-sighted, and a systematic policy framework was needed. From this point onwards, worldwide, central banks started to re-design their policy framework to avoid repetition of the aforementioned situation.

In the aftermath of the Volcker Shock, it was essential to design the framework. The Taylor Rule, proposed first by John Taylor in 1993, was the first tool that linked the policy rate to the deviations of inflation and output from target. Equation (2.1) presents the rule:

---

[1] The news was reported in several media outlets. See: https://www.reuters.com/markets/us/stagflation-radar-us-economy-no-repeat-70s-2025-03-25/?utm_source=chatgpt.com

[2] Here's how forecasters saw U.S. inflation for 1979:

- **Federal Reserve staff (Greenbook, Dec 1978)**

  In its December 1978 projection, the Fed's economics "Greenbook" raised its forecast for the coming year to about **7¾ percent** inflation—measured by the fixed-weighted price index for gross business product—roughly one percentage point below the prior year's rise (Greenbook Part 1 - Federal Reserve Board).

- **Private-sector consensus (early-1979 surveys)**

  Retrospective compilations of private forecasts (often associated with the Blue Chip consensus) show economists expecting around **12.0 percent** CPI-type inflation for 1979, compared with a n

  actual rate of 13.3 percent (Historical U.S. Inflation Rate by Year: 1929 to 2025 - Investopedia).

- **University of Michigan Survey of Consumers (early 1979)**

  Long-run inflation expectations among consumers rose to about **7 percent** by the start of 1979, up from roughly 5 percent in 1977 ([PDF] The Great Inflation - National Bureau of Economic Research).

In short, forecasts in late 1978 and early 1979 ranged from roughly 7–8 per cent in official Greenbook and consumer surveys to about 12 percent in private-sector projections—underestimating the 13.3 per cent inflation that actually occurred.

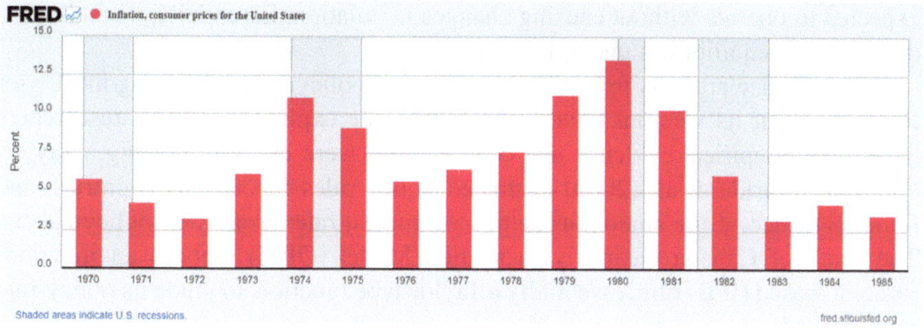

Fig. 2.1 CPI for the United States. The figure presents the level of inflation as the yearly variation of the Consumer Price Index the United States. Source: World Bank via FRED

$$i_t = r^* + \pi_t + 0.5\left(\pi_t - \pi^*\right) + 0.5\left(y_t - y^*\right) \tag{2.1}$$

where:

- i_t is the nominal interest rate (the Federal Funds Rate) in %
- r^* is the equilibrium rate, often set at 2%[3]
- π_t is the rate of inflation (% change in the GDP deflator)
- π^* is the target rate of inflation, 2% for most central banks (FED, Bank of England, European Central Bank among others).
- $y_t - y^*$ is the output gap. The deviation of the current output, generally approximated with GDP from its potential.

The output gap was and is rather complicated to measure, given the aleatory nature of the "potential output" part of the equation. Despite the straightforward nature of this policy rule, it still was rather complicated to be directly applied by policymakers.

Rudebusch (2010) published a version of the rule that utilized unemployment instead of output, which was and still is more in line with the mandate of the FED, which has as aim the achievement of full employment.

$$i_t = 1.25 + 1.5\left(\pi_t\right) - 2\left(u_t - u^*\right) \tag{2.2}$$

where:

i_t is the nominal interest rate (the Federal Funds Rate) in %

π_t is the core rate of inflation

$u_t - u^*$ is the unemployment rate minus the Non-Accelerating Inflation Rate of Unemployment, a theoretical level of unemployment at which the economy is

[3] The equilibrium interest rate varies across central banks and countries. For example, it is often set at 2% for the United States and 2.75% for the United Kingdom.

expected to operate without causing changes in inflation. Essentially, it can be also defined as an equilibrium unemployment rate.

Although declarations from central banks and policymakers of using the Taylor Rule or one of its versions have never been made explicit, academic researchers have found empirical evidence that central banks were in fact following a Taylor-type rule. Clarida et al. (2000) estimated policy rules for various countries, and found evidence of the analogous setting of interest rates from their policymakers. The Bank of Canada Quarterly Projection Model (QPM) embeds an inflation-forecast–based (IFB) rule, essentially a Taylor-type function, to guide its policy-rate projections.[4]

At the same time, the practical success of Inflation Targeting (IT) frameworks in New Zealand in 1990 convinced other countries to follow: Canada (1991), the United Kingdom (1992), Sweden and Australia (1993), the Eurozone (2003), and Japan (2013). Under inflation targeting, central banks make a public commitment to a numeric inflation goal (typically around 2 per cent), publish regular Monetary Policy Reports and minutes, and explain deviations in "open and accountable" fora. IT frameworks, made essential a dramatic change into the communication policies of central banks (more on this will be discussed in the following Chap. 3).

The IT adoption coincided with a period of economic stability often referred to as the "Great Moderation". From the mid-1980s to the early 2000s, advanced economies saw both inflation and output volatility decline to multi-decade lows. Anchored expectations, improved inventory management in supply chains, and the disinflationary effects of globalization all played roles. However, this tranquillity masked a build-up of financial imbalances. The low-interest rate environment caused a risk shift in investors an asset price boom, more evident in housing, fostering also a rapid credit growth.

Lately, this period will be referred to as a global savings glut, as emerging market economies accumulated large current surpluses and reallocated this cash into advanced-economy debt markets. China, prior to the 2008 financial crisis, was, in fact, holding about 421 billion of US Treasuries.[5]

When U.S. house-price declines in 2006 triggered a cascade of mortgage delinquencies, funding markets seized up in 2007, culminating in the collapse of Lehman Brothers in September 2008 and the deepest financial crisis since the 1930s. With policy rates at or near the zero-lower bound (ZLB), central banks pioneered unconventional responses: large-scale asset purchases (quantitative easing), term liquidity facilities, forward guidance anchored on labour-market outcomes, and extensive currency-swap networks to provide dollar funding overseas.

More recently, central banks have faced exogenous shocks beyond the traditional business cycle: the political disruption of Brexit, which rocked sterling and business confidence; the COVID-19 pandemic, which brought global economic activity to a

[4] Studies actually found that Taylor-type rules track the overnight interest rates of the Bank of Canada.

[5] www.everycrsreport.com/files/20080227_RL34314_d574a341450221672e81291cd21df14f7ebb9d41.pdf

near-complete halt; and subsequent supply-chain bottlenecks that have reignited inflationary pressures. In each episode, policymakers have had to adapt their frameworks and toolkits, often pushing the boundaries of their mandates and raising enduring questions about the appropriate division of labour between monetary, fiscal, and macroprudential authorities.

This chapter traces that evolution in three stages:

1. Inflation Pressures and Policy Frameworks: From the Great Inflation to the Great Moderation.
2. The 2008 Financial Crisis. We analyse monetary settings that contributed to the housing boom, the Fed's pioneering early responses, the delayed but eventual interventions by the European Central Bank and Bank of England, and the debate over whether policy should more systematically respond to financial-market signals.
3. Exogenous Shocks: We examine how Brexit and the COVID-19 pandemic forced policymakers to innovate beyond conventional frameworks.

Although early to say, current policy tariffs in the United States will also challenge the modus operandi of the Federal Reserve, along with international conflict. Further work should look at these additional shocks.

2.2 Inflation Pressures and Monetary Policy: From the Great Inflation to Systemic Reform

When the Bretton Woods system collapsed in 1971, a period of floating currencies and high volatility in commodities began. In 1973, the Global Price shock of the oil embargo (300% increment in oil price per barrel) resulted in a sudden jump in energy costs (about 70% in one year), and core consumer price inflation across OECD countries jumped to over 8 per cent by the end of 1974. Central banks tried to keep prices under control by tightening interest rates (up to almost 13% around 1974), and just afterwards reversed their policy to support a weakening output and labour market (down to 5.5% in 1975). This period was called the "stop-go" cycle by Milton Friedman (among others). Essentially, the Federal Funds rate varied by almost 7% within less than a couple of years. Output resumed, however, inflation climbed up to 12% in 1979,[6] leaving high concerns about price stability (Goodfriend, 2007).

The concerns about inflation inspired the need for a price stability framework and the necessity of anchoring expectations. Inflation pressures around the world convinced policymakers that a more systematic approach was needed. High volatility in interest rates led to a harsh economic period in the US. At the end of the

[6]Other countries experienced even sharper climbs, for example the UK inflation nearly reached 20%.

1980s, countries around the world started to embrace the pioneering regime of New Zealand. New Zealand, in 1989, became the first country to adopt a formal inflation targeting framework.

The New Zealand central bank, agreed with the government to:

- *Inflation Target*: Maintain CPI inflation between 0 and 2 per cent.
- *Policy Horizon*: Return inflation to target "over the medium term", recognizing lags in policy transmission.
- *Transparency:* Publish quarterly Monetary Policy Statements with detailed forecasts of inflation and output.
- *Accountability:* Report to Parliament and submit to ministerial review if targets were missed.

An explicit numerical anchor was necessary for several reasons, and particularly to anchor public beliefs and expectations. With slightly different targets or inflation ranges, more central banks joined the framework. Canada followed suit in 1991 (1–3 per cent CPI), the U.K. in 1992 (2.5 per cent target on the RPIX measure), and Sweden and Australia in 1993 (2 per cent and 2–3 per cent CPI, respectively). By the mid-1990s, inflation targeting was the dominant regime among advanced economies, covering over half of global GDP.

The core elements of an Inflation targeting framework are therefore: (1) an explicit numeric target for inflation, which as noted is often expressed around 2% and may be symmetric around the value; (2) a medium-term orientation to recognize the lag in the effect of monetary policy. This horizon will also avoid the reaction to short-term shocks, such as shocks in commodities. The policy instruments employed are typically the policy interest rates (e.g. the Federal Funds rate, Bank Rate); (4) the communication and transparency that accompanies it; (5) institutional independence and accountability measures (e.g., publications of minutes and record).

Given the success in multiple countries, it is worth discussing the operational side of the inflation targeting framework. This modus operandi of aligning tools to achieve the price stability goal, the forward guidance in the communication, and the acknowledgement that monetary policy affects the economy with a time lag (Svensson, 2003), forced central banks to implement a forecast-based decision-making process. In other words, current or ex-post data are not the food for thought of policymakers; forecasts are.[7] This information are used and processed by a committee of individuals, who use them to manage the monetary policy tool (e.g., the Federal Open Market Committee, FOMC, in the US). The framework is ultimately embedded in a reaction function, which could look like the aforementioned Taylor Rule.

In the following table, we discuss the advantages and disadvantages of the framework, summarizing key points found in seminal academic literature on the topic (Table 2.1).

[7] This latter element had important implications for the academic research that focused on estimating the wanted and unwanted impact of monetary policy (Romer & Romer, 1998, 2004, 2023), which will be further discussed in Chaps. 4 and 5.

Table 2.1 Pros and cons of inflation targeting framework

Advantages	Disadvantages
1. *Anchoring of inflation expectations & reduced volatility* By committing to a clear target, central banks can better anchor long-run inflation expectations, which empirically leads to lower inflation persistence and smaller swings in both inflation and output.	1. *Perceived narrow focus & "inflation nutter" risk* If misinterpreted as a strict rule, inflation targeting can be seen as neglecting real--economy objectives, leading to criticism.
2. *Enhances Transparency & Accountability* Public targets and reporting make it easier to judge central bank performance. Allows also the public to be included in the discussion and better understand the reasoning behind the policies.	2. *High institutional & operational requirements* A successful framework demands central bank independence, absence of fiscal dominance, deep financial markets, high-quality data, and forecasting capacity. All of these elements might need time to be built in a country.
3. *Policy discipline through "constrained discretion"* Strike a balance between rigid rules and unfettered discretion ("constrained discretion"), enhancing policy discipline while still allowing judgment in the face of shocks.	3. *Mixed empirical macroeconomic benefits* Recent surveys find that, especially in advanced economies, inflation targeting's gains in reducing inflation persistence or improving output growth are modest and not always statistically significant.
4. *Flexibility to stabilize output as well as prices* Although focused on price stability, most inflation targeting regimes explicitly allow for "flexible" targeting—Responding to both inflation and output gaps—Which helps mitigate trade-offs during economic disturbances.	4. *Reliance on accurate forecasts & measurement* Effectiveness hinges on the ability to forecast inflation and choose the right price index (headline vs. core); forecasting errors or misspecification of the target variable can lead to policy missteps.
5. *Improved implementation & monitoring* Using forecasts of inflation as an intermediate target streamlines policy implementation and performance monitoring, making it easier to adjust instruments proactively.	5. *Challenges at the zero-lower bound* When policy rates approach zero, forward--looking inflation targeting may fail to anchor expectations at the chosen target, creating a downward bias in inflation forecasts.

Sources: Author elaboration of Bernanke and Mishkin (1997), Bernanke (2003), Freedman and Laxton (2009), Freedman and Ötker-Robe (2009), Freedman and Ötker-Robe (2010), Svensson (1997)

The IT framework sparked additional criticisms and limitations in the wake of the 2007–08 financial crisis. Particularly, the focus on merely the Consumer Price Index (CPI) could create some blind spots in relation to financial stability. For example, rapid increases in housing or equity prices could lead to bubbles and financial instability, yet CPI could remain unchanged for longer. A more flexible approach could support lower market volatility (Cecchetti et al., 2002). Additionally, in low inflation environments and sparking financial innovation, credit booms can fuel bubbles even more (Borio & Lowe, 2002). These last two concerns were initially marginal; only after the crisis, they became central and led to discussion on how to include financial stability in the mandate of central banks.

2.3 From the Great Inflation to the 2008 Financial Crisis

By the mid-1980s, inflation was tamed and the volatility of GDP growth had also considerably declined. This period of the *"Great Moderation"* was attributed to improved monetary policy that benefitted from IT frameworks, structural changes in financial regulation and globalization, and fewer commodities shocks. As Bernanke (2004) argues, the striking feature of this period is the decline in macroeconomic volatility. We provide an example of this by looking at the CPI of the United States in two-time intervals, (1970–1986) and (1986–2007). Both the average level and the standard deviations are less than one half in the time period that was defined as the Great Moderation (Table 2.2).

Whatever its root cause, the Great Moderation fostered a sense that macroeconomic stability was here to stay, until the realization that financial imbalances were quietly mounting. The anchoring of expectations has allowed nominal interest rates to drift in the low region. Additionally, the DotCom Bubble pushed the interest rates even lower.

As shown in Fig. 2.2, between 2000 and 2001, interest rates dropped, creating imbalances after 2002. In 2006, $800 billion was the US and other advanced economies' deficit, whilst oil-exporters, China and Japan's surplus was slightly higher (Davies, 2014). A number of personalities attributed part of the financial crisis blame to these global imbalances in the years that preceded the crisis (Obstfeld & Rogoff, 2009; Borio & Disyatat, 2010; Obstfeld, 2012). Bernanke (2005) introduced the term "global saving glut" to describe how elevated saving rates in emerging Asia and oil-exporting countries, driven by precautionary motives and the desire to build reserves, created an excess supply of loanable funds.

Ultimately, a low interest rates environment will lead to shifts in risk preferences and flights of funds towards higher yield investments. In the absence of yields, the financial industry innovated. The innovation arrived timely with the boom of the housing market in the US, after several social policies to support Americans families in affording a home. To make this feasible, deregulation came first. Beginning with the Alternative Mortgage Transaction Parity Act (1982) and continuing through the Garn-St Germain Act (1982) and the Gramm-Leach-Bliley Act (1999), restrictions on adjustable-rate and exotic mortgage contracts were lifted. This deregulation fostered the originate-to-distribute model: lenders could originate nontraditional mortgages and then offload them to investors (Coval et al., 2009).

The Housing and Community Development Act of 1992 charged Fannie Mae and Freddie Mac with purchasing a rising share of "affordable" mortgages. The combined affordable-housing goals rose from 30 per cent in 1992 to over 50 per cent by 2000. To meet these quotas, the GSEs increasingly guaranteed, and in turn

Table 2.2 Average CPI United States

	Average	St. Dev
1970–1985	7.00	3.22
1986–2007	3.03	1.07

Source: OECD data

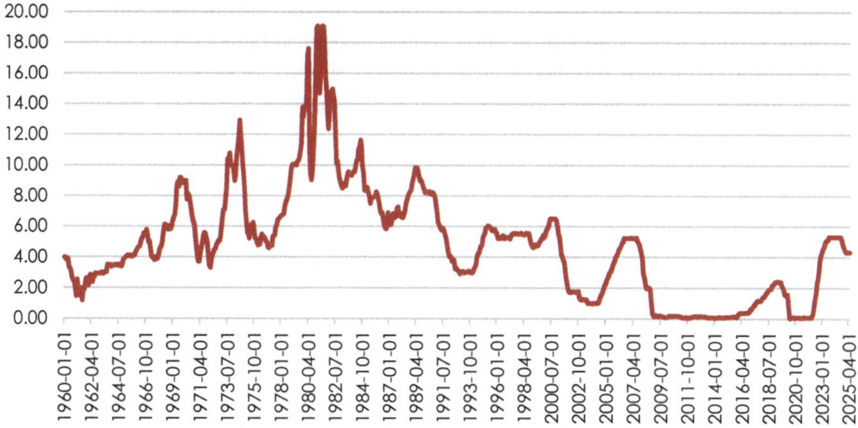

Fig. 2.2 Federal funds rate. The graph presents the level of the Federal Funds Target rate from the 01/1960 until 04/2025. Source: FRED

securitized, subprime and Alt-A loans, effectively channelling riskier mortgages into the secondary market (Glaeser et al., 2010).

These policies dramatically expanded the supply of mortgage credit and laid the groundwork for the rapid growth of mortgage-backed securities (MBS). As lenders securitized an ever-larger share of originations, they lost incentives in screening borrowers. The risk was sold right after it was taken. This also made it more complicated during and after the crisis when it was necessary to understand the sources of risk. Empirical work shows that the originate-to-distribute chain led to systematically laxer underwriting standards in subprime lending (Keys et al., 2010). Moreover, the surge in securitization itself acted as a credit-supply shock: new homebuyers were financed by loans that, once originated, were immediately pooled, tranched, and sold to investors, fuelling both the housing boom and the subsequent spikes in delinquency (Mian & Sufi, 2009). Structured-finance tranching and credit enhancements obscured true risk profiles, concentrating exposures within shadow-banking conduits and amplifying systemic vulnerability (Coval et al., 2009; Demyanyk & Van Hemert, 2011). According to the Securities Industry and Financial Markets Association's US Credit Market Outlook 2007 (February 1, 2007),[8] U.S. issuance of MBS and CDOs in 2007 was approximately $2.07 trillion and $369 billion, respectively.

Credit default swaps (CDS) allowed sophisticated hedging and speculative trades on corporate and structured-product credit risk. CDS were the insurance product paired up with CDOs and traded by the same entities. When structured products started to default and lose their value, the CDS were triggered, causing even more systematic risk. All together, the strong appreciation in house prices worldwide (in

[8] Securities Industry and Financial Markets Association. (2007, February 1). US credit market outlook 2007. Retrieved from https://www.sifma.org/resources/research/economics/us-credit-market-outlook-2007

the US house prices rose about 55%, according to the S&P/Case-Shiller Index). Credit to GDP almost doubled by 2007, however central banks did not have a case for pre-emptive interest rate hikes, as headline CPI was not enough risen and they did not identify the bubble rising either. In 2004, Federal Reserve Chairman Alan Greenspan remarked that identifying "bubbles" would require tools that central banks did not possess and that pre-emptive rate tightening to deflate asset prices would risk harming the broader economy.

This reluctance to use policy rates to target asset-price inflation meant that, even as the ratio of household debt to disposable income and the ratio of real estate valuations to rental yields soared, official interest rates remained accommodative. Only in late 2005 did the Fed begin to raise rates, incrementally lifting the federal funds rate from 1 per cent to 5.25 per cent by mid-2006. By then, housing leverage had peaked, but vulnerabilities embedded in mortgage servicing pipelines, CDO warehouse lines, and funding-dependent dealers were already acute.

2.4 The Response to the Crisis

The crisis emerged in mid-2007, when the U.S. subprime mortgage sector experienced rising delinquencies and write-downs in structured credit products. In August 2007, BNP Paribas froze redemptions in three of its funds, citing an "inability to value certain assets".[9] A correction of the housing market quickly became a systematic meltdown of the credit markets, banking system, and financial markets. Central banks had to deal with more than one issue at the same time. Being concentrated on core inflation for the past decade, their tools were limited with interest rates that left little margins of movements and a new enemy: financial stability (Oosterloo & De Haan, 2004).

Whether financial stability should be part of central banks' mandate had become a central question in the aftermath of the financial crisis for both academics and practitioners, after the discovery of the systemic nature of the banking system. When asked to the public, the financial crisis is often identified with the bankruptcy of Lehman Brothers and its consequences. Interestingly enough, the meltdown of Lehman will also remain debated as to whether it had excessive consequences and should have been avoided, which brings us to the second enemy that emerged from the crisis: moral hazard.

The response to the financial crisis was a series of interest rate cuts in the US and further the development of "unconventional monetary policy tools". Unconventional monetary policies are a set of tools used by central banks when the targeting of interest rates or reserves is no longer a viable option. In the early 2000s, the Bank of Japan first implemented a large-scale quantitative easing (QE) (Matousek et al., 2019), which provided empirical evidence and a case for the employment by other

[9] https://www.reuters.com/article/markets/funds/bnp-freezes-22-bln-of-funds-over-subprime-idUSGRI926030/

countries in other circumstances. One of the central debated aspects of QE programs is that central banks had to work through financial markets directly. This aspect raised several questions about the involvement of central banks in the markets and unwanted repercussions.

Janet Yellen had to clarify more than once that the FED would have worked through financial markets and not for (or in favour) of financial markets. Yet, fears of the development of moral hazard remained even after the meltdown of Lehman. The further intervention of the US government and the creation of the Troubled Asset Relief Program (TARP) made it evident that institutional intervention was needed. The TARP ultimately provided capital to over 500 firms, mostly major banks and insurance companies. Key recipients (among many) included: Citigroup, Bank of America, JPMorgan Chase, Wells Fargo, Goldman Sachs, Morgan Stanley, and American International Group (AIG). Roughly $426 billion was made available and provided a net profit of $15.3 billion. Additional arguments in the literature were made on the changes in banks' valuation, following the TARP program. Veronesi and Zingales (2010) estimated that it increased the value of banks' financial claims by $130 billion at a taxpayers' cost of $21–$44 billion. They infer that this net benefit comes from a significant reduction in the probability of bankruptcy. Bayazitova and Shivdasani (2011) provided empirical evidence of the financial market impact of the announcements of the TARP.

Central banks, along with their QE programs, started to implement additional unconventional monetary policy tools. Among others, *"forward guidance"* was introduced along with other strong improvements to the communication skills and tools employed by the policymakers. The aim is to give statements about the future path of interest rates, to shape market expectations and further influence long-term yields. An example is the famous "Evans Rule" that stated that rates would remain exceptionally low until unemployment fell below 6.5 per cent (based on the Phillips-Curve projection for the core PCE deflator one to two years ahead). This marked a clear shift from purely time-based guidance ("at least through late 2014") towards state-contingent (or "Odyssean") forward guidance, designed to strengthen the Fed's promise of extended accommodation even as economic conditions improved. Campbell et al. (2012) show in a DSGE framework that such threshold-based conditioning can meaningfully lower both short- and long-term rates by managing expectations credibly, while Chung et al. (2012) demonstrate via FRB/US simulations that explicit liftoff rules materially reduce the risk of prematurely tightening at the zero-lower bound. Empirically, Nakamura and Steinsson (2018) use high-frequency identification to confirm that FOMC statements containing clear, quantitative guidance materially affect Treasury yields, underscoring the potency of the Evans Rule's explicit thresholds. Similarly, the ECB committed to hold rates at low level (in 2013) and clearly communicated that. The BOE also specified that the Bank Rate would not rise above 1%, until unemployment was below 7%. These conditional forward guidance frameworks were designed to lower yields by convincing markets that policy would stay loose even after visible signs of recovery, thereby providing additional accommodation beyond zero rates.

The overall response of the ECB and BOE was somehow different and delayed. The United Kingdom, for example, used a similar rescue package that saved institutions such as the Royal Bank of Scotland with a total injection of about £45.8 billion. Mixed evidence on their benefits was found by further literature (Brei et al., 2013). The ECB, in particular, bound by its founding treaty to maintain "price stability" (interpreted as HICP inflation "below, but close to, 2 per cent"), initially hesitated to embark on large asset purchases. Its early crisis tools included: Longer-Term Refinancing Operations (LTROs), the Covered Bond Purchase Programme (CBPP), and the Securities Markets Programme (SMP).

Despite these steps, outright QE comparable to the Fed's was delayed until January 2015, when the ECB launched its Public Sector Purchase Programme (PSPP) and Corporate Sector Purchase Programme (CSPP), committing to €60 billion per month in bond purchases (Runkel, 2022). The LTROs started in late 2008 and the ECB offered three-month and six-month loans at fixed rates, absorbing excess liquidity in the banking system. The CBPP, from summer 2009, supported market liquidity as the ECB was buying covered bonds. A year after, in May 2010, the ECB announced purchases of peripheral sovereign debt (Greece, Ireland, Portugal, Spain) to restore orderly markets. The effectiveness and repercussions of these programs were widely studied in the literature with mixed results (Joyce & Tong, 2012; Gambacorta et al., 2014; Eser & Schwaab, 2016; Altavilla et al., 2021).

It is worth mentioning that these interventions in Europe were not only tackling the meltdown caused by the 2008 financial crisis but also the sovereign debt crisis that followed up very shortly. The global financial shock forced European governments to bail out banks, which in turn sharply raised public debt and seeded a vicious sovereign–bank loop. First, bank rescue packages, by transferring contingent liabilities onto sovereign balance sheets, heightened sovereign credit risk and undermined banks' collateral (Acharya et al., 2014). Second, sovereign distress fed back into the banking sector, further contracting credit supply and deepening the recession (Gennaioli et al., 2014). Third, financial markets, which had largely ignored sovereign fundamentals before 2008, began to demand large risk premia as fiscal positions diverged and contagion spread from Greece to Ireland, Portugal, Spain, and beyond (Beirne & Fratzscher, 2013). Fourth, in the absence of a euro-area lender of last resort, self-fulfilling liquidity runs on peripheral sovereigns materialized in 2010–11, amplifying yields independently of fundamental fiscal metrics (De Grauwe & Ji, 2013). Lastly, the Eurozone lacked centralized fiscal supports and a unified crisis management, leading to the full-blown sovereign-debt crisis by 2011 (Lane, 2012).

2.5 Exogenous Shocks

Although endogeneity is at the heart of macroeconomic analysis and monetary policy is embedded in the endogenous relationships of macroeconomic variables such as inflation and unemployment, a few exogenous shocks have required the intervention of monetary policymakers. Central banks operate primarily with the business-cycle in mind, targeting fluctuations in output and inflation. Yet truly exogenous shocks, such as political ruptures, health crises, and supply-chain disruptions, can thrust policymakers into uncharted territory. This section examines two such episodes: Brexit and the COVID-19 pandemic. The current turmoil related to US tariffs under the Trump administration would also be worth including in this discussion. However, the evidence is yet limited. We believe this would be part of further interesting studies and advancement in the literature.

2.5.1 A Political Shock: Brexit

On June 23, 2016, the United Kingdom voted 52 per cent to 48 per cent to leave the European Union. Financial markets reacted violently: sterling fell by over 8 per cent against the dollar in a single trading session, the FTSE 100 index dropped 3.5 per cent, and volatility indices spiked to multi-year highs. Figure 2.3 depicts what happened within that week and with the further interest rate cut that happened on the 4th of August 2016.

The figure shows the dynamics of the stock market and the Bank Rate. What is interesting to notice is the negative reaction of the FTSE 100 Index, the UK main equity index, on the Brexit announcement day and the positive response on the days after the Bank Rate cut. In line with theory,[10] financial markets respond to the arrival of information, a negative shock with Brexit, however, a positive shock when interest rates are cut and better conditions materialize for companies' cost of debt. The

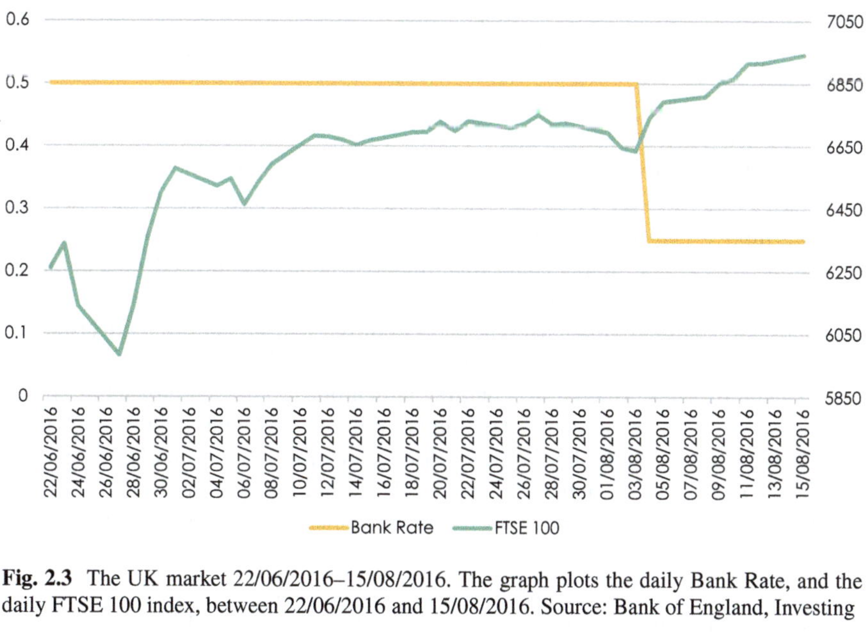

Fig. 2.3 The UK market 22/06/2016–15/08/2016. The graph plots the daily Bank Rate, and the daily FTSE 100 index, between 22/06/2016 and 15/08/2016. Source: Bank of England, Investing

[10] Financial markets dynamics and monetary policy will be further discussed in Chaps. 4 and 5.

level of financial market uncertainty spiked, as also noticed in the VIX index. Along with the August interest rate cut from 0.5% to 0.25%, the BOE increased the stock of UK government bond purchases to £435 billion,[11] and added £10 billion of corporate bond purchases. Forward guidance was also largely employed, with clear statements from the BOE that reiterated that the Bank Rate would have remained at its lower bound until they were confident of contained inflation. The intention was to stabilize the markets, ease financial conditions, and provide a buffer in the case of adverse movements in UK GDP. The recent work of Geiger and Güntner (2024) found empirical evidence that the accommodative monetary policy of the BOE prevented an even stronger output effect. What is extremely interesting and important in this piece of research is the complete reporting of not only the announcement itself, but also the series of political announcements on the withdrawal that followed and were as unanticipated as the decision itself.

Brexit highlighted how political events—outside the control of monetary authorities—can trigger substantial currency and confidence shocks. It also underscored the limits of monetary policy: once interest rates hit the lower bound, further support requires coordination with fiscal authorities, regulatory forbearance, or broader "macro support" measures.

2.5.2 A Completely Unforeseen Scenario: COVID-19

In late 2019, reports of a novel coronavirus in Wuhan, China, began to surface. By January 2020, SARS-CoV-2 had spread internationally, and the World Health Organization declared a Public Health Emergency of International Concern on January 30. At the beginning of March, most governments around the world enacted lockdowns, travel bans, and social-distancing measures that brought large swaths of economic activity to an abrupt halt.

Covid-19 was an unprecedented event that involved, unlike traditional cyclical downturns, the COVID-19 shock combined simultaneous supply and demand shocks. Supply shut down, with factories being closed and service sector ceasing operations. The global supply chain was fractured, causing unprecedented damages to international trade. On the demand side, household consumption plunged as people sheltered. Unemployment surged, firms deferred investments, and governments had to intervene to support the latter and avoid the total freeze of the economy.

Financial markets, as leading economic indicators, did not anticipate this shock, or at least not in its actual depth. The market plunged in March 2020 as lockdown news spread across the globe, liquidity dried up as the funding market froze, and volatility spiked to levels unheard of before. The rapidity and synchronicity of these shocks left no historical playbook. Central banks had to react within days,

[11] See Bank of England "Inflation Report" of August 2016 for details on the response to Brexit (www.bankofengland.co.uk/-/media/boe/files/inflation-report/2016/august-2016.pdf)

deploying every tool available to prevent a collapse in credit intermediation and a permanent loss of productive capacity.

The first move from the Federal Reserve was a series of interest rate cuts that more or less wiped out all the interest rate recovery that happened after the zero-lower bound period. The FOMC convened on March 3rd, 15th, and 23rd 2020 and cut 100 bps of interest rates altogether. On top of the interest rate cuts, they activated swap lines with nine major central banks at unlimited amounts and announced plans to purchase Treasury and agency mortgage-backed securities (MBS) "in the amounts needed to support smooth market functioning".[12]

The ECB followed a similar path and cut the Main Refinancing Operations rate (MRO) by 50 basis points on the 12th of March and launched a further Pandemic Emergency Purchase Programme (PEPP), earmarked for public and private-sector securities, with flexible reinvestment criteria. The program started at €750 billion and the Governing Council further increased it by €600 billion on 4 June 2020 and by €500 billion on 10 December 2020, to a new total of €1850 billion. All asset categories eligible for purchase under the existing asset purchase programme (APP) were also eligible under the PEPP, and the eligibility requirements were waived for securities issued by the Greek Government.[13]

The BOE also acted swiftly and cut the Bank Rate on the 11th and on the 19th of March to 0.1%, the effective lower bound. The Asset Purchase Facility was expanded by £200 billion (bringing total QE to £645 billion), and established the Term Funding Scheme with additional incentives for SMEs. Collectively, the simultaneous interventions of the central banks far exceeded the efforts and scale of moves of those of 2008, reflecting the uniqueness and severity of the pandemic shock.

2.5.3 *Post COVID-19 Economy*

By mid-2021, life and the economy seemed ready to be "back to usual business". The unprecedented rollout of the vaccination plans worldwide allowed schools, businesses, and travel to resume without the fear that the healthcare system could collapse again. The economy rebounded, thanks also to various support plans, such as the generous fiscal stimulus in the US (American Rescue Plan Act). The pace and shape of recovery varied around the world. The US had a fast paced recovery thanks to a robust consumer demand and a strong housing market, with GDP growing at nearly 6% in the second quarter of 2021. The Euro-Area, the old continent, moved at a slower pace due to the slower vaccine rollout, structural rigidities, and uneven fiscal support. Growth in mid-2021 hovered around 2–3 per cent annualized.

---

[12] For details, see: https://www.federalreserve.gov/newsevents/pressreleases/monetary20200315c.htm

[13] For details, see: https://www.ecb.europa.eu/mopo/implement/pepp/html/index.en.html

The UK bounced back strongly in Q2 2021, aided by successful vaccination and pent-up spending, however, Brexit-related frictions were still echoing and complicating the situation, particularly for everything concerning trade and the supply chain of goods. The heterogeneity in the response of different geographical areas made it more challenging for policymakers to coordinate monetary policy actions.

What really has characterized the post-COVID economy are the supply chain disruptions, the inflationary pressures, and the rise in international conflicts. The supply was struggling to keep up with the demand, given the damage caused by factory shutdowns and the rising imbalances in the shipping industry.[14]

All of these factors contributed to the rise in inflation that exceeded 7% over year change in the US by December 2021. Core inflation measures worldwide—excluding food and energy—also climbed, signalling more generalized price pressures. Central banks initially described the spike in inflation as "transitory", driven by base effects and one-off supply disruptions. However, as price pressures persisted into 2022, driven further by energy-price surges following Russia's invasion of Ukraine, policymakers faced criticism for underestimating the persistence of inflation dynamics.

By mid-2022 the hike in inflation normalized and required the control of central banks. The FED re-initiated the raising of interest rates and brought them to a more neutral level between 2.5 and 3%. The ECB shut down the PEPP purchases by March 2022 and implemented the first hike of interest rates in July 2022, by raising the deposit rate to the 0% level (from −0.5%). The BOE commenced the rate increases in December 2021 (15 basis points), followed by multiple hikes bringing the Bank Rate to 1.25 per cent by mid-2022, alongside a modest reduction in the stock of purchased gilts.

Policymakers, in the aftermath of the pandemic crisis, were now faced with additional and different queries. The queries were mainly related to effectively manage the expansion of the central banks' balance sheets. Mandates and related communication were again challenged. The new inflation level required a revision of the guidance for the public when inflation remains elevated, growth slows, and stagflation risk arises again.

The pandemic has made us rethink the world, everyday life, and naturally pushed for an appraisal of the monetary framework. Central banks' mandate may need to be expanded beyond inflation and unemployment and further into financial stability and exogenous shocks.

[14] The damages made to the labour market made it more difficult to rehire the labor force needed to satisfy the demand. Additionally, shipping bottlenecks and congestion in major ports complicated the situation (Stevenson, 2020; Van Doornik et al., 2023)

References

Acharya, V. V., Drechsler, I., & Schnabl, P. (2014). A Pyrrhic victory? Bank bailouts and sovereign credit risk. *Journal of Finance, 69*(6), 2689–2739.

Altavilla, C., Carboni, G., & Motto, R. (2021). Asset purchase programs and financial markets: Lessons from the Euro Area. *International Journal of Central Banking, 17*(4), 1–48.

Bayazitova, D., & Shivdasani, A. (2011). Assessing TARP. *Review of Financial Studies, 25*(2), 377–407.

Beirne, J., & Fratzscher, M. (2013). The pricing of sovereign risk and contagion during the European sovereign debt crisis. *Journal of International Money and Finance, 34*, 60–82.

Bernanke, B. S. (2003). A perspective on inflation targeting. *Business Economics, 38*(3).

Bernanke, B. S. (2005, April 14). *The global saving glut and the U.S. current account deficit.* Homer Jones Lecture.

Bernanke, B. S., & Mishkin, F. S. (1997). Inflation targeting: A new framework for monetary policy? *Journal of Economic Perspectives, 11*(2), 97–116.

Borio, C., & Disyatat, P. (2010). Global imbalances and the financial crisis: Reassessing the role of international finance. *Asian Economic Policy Review, 5*(2), 198–216.

Borio, C., & Lowe, P. (2002). *Asset prices, financial and monetary stability: Exploring the nexus. BIS working paper no. 114.* Bank for International Settlements.

Brei, M., Gambacorta, L., & Von Peter, G. (2013). Rescue packages and bank lending. *Journal of Banking & Finance, 37*(2), 490–505.

Campbell, J. R., Evans, C. L., Fisher, J. D. M., & Justiniano, A. (2012). Macroeconomic effects of Federal Reserve forward guidance. *Brookings Papers on Economic Activity, Spring*, 1–80.

Cecchetti, S. G., Genberg, H., & Wadhwani, S. (2002). *Asset prices in a flexible inflation targeting framework.* NBER Working Paper, (w8970).

Chung, H., Laforte, J.-P., Reifschneider, D., & Williams, J. C. (2012). Have we underestimated the likelihood and severity of zero lower bound events? *Journal of Money, Credit and Banking, 44*(1), 47–82.

Clarida, R. H., Galí, J., & Gertler, M. (2000). Monetary policy rules and macroeconomic stability: Evidence and some theory. *The Quarterly Journal of Economics, 115*(1), 147–180.

Coval, J., Jurek, J. W., & Stafford, E. (2009). The economics of structured finance. *Journal of Economic Perspectives, 23*(1), 3–25.

Davies, H. (2014). *The financial crisis: Who is to blame?* Wiley.

De Grauwe, P., & Ji, Y. (2013). Self-fulfilling crises in the Eurozone: An empirical test. *Journal of International Money and Finance, 34*, 15–36.

Demyanyk, Y., & Van Hemert, O. (2011). Understanding the subprime mortgage crisis. *Review of Financial Studies, 24*(6), 1848–1880.

Eser, F., & Schwaab, B. (2016). Evaluating the impact of unconventional monetary policy measures: Empirical evidence from the ECB's securities markets Programme. *Journal of Financial Economics, 119*(1), 147–167.

Freedman, C., & Laxton, M. D. (2009). *Why inflation targeting? (No. 2009/086).* International Monetary Fund.

Freedman, C., & Ötker-Robe, I. (2009). *Country experiences with the introduction and implementation of inflation targeting*. IMF Working Paper 09/161.

Freedman, C., & Ötker-Robe, I. (2010). *Important elements for inflation targeting for emerging economies*. IMF Working Paper 10/113.

Gambacorta, L., Hofmann, B., & Peersman, G. (2014). The effectiveness of unconventional monetary policy at the zero lower bound: A cross-country analysis. *Journal of Money, Credit and Banking, 46*(4), 615–642.

Geiger, M., & Güntner, J. (2024). The chronology of Brexit and UK monetary policy. *Journal of Monetary Economics, 142*, 103516.

Gennaioli, N., Martin, A., & Rossi, S. (2014). Sovereign default, domestic banks, and financial institutions. *Journal of Finance, 69*(2), 819–866.

Glaeser, E. L., Gottlieb, J. D., & Gyourko, J. (2010). Did government intervention fuel the housing boom? *Journal of Monetary Economics, 57*(1), 15–32.

Goodfriend, M. S. (2007). How the world achieved consensus on monetary policy. *Journal of Economic Perspectives, 21*(4), 47–68.

Joyce, M. A. S., & Tong, M. (2012). QE and the gilt market: A disaggregated analysis. *Economic Journal, 122*(564), 348–384.

Keys, B. J., Mukherjee, T., Seru, A., & Vig, V. (2010). Did securitization lead to lax screening? Evidence from subprime loans. *Quarterly Journal of Economics, 125*(1), 307–362.

Lane, P. R. (2012). The European sovereign debt crisis. *Journal of Economic Perspectives, 26*(3), 49–68.

Matousek, R., Papadamou, S. T., Šević, A., & Tzeremes, N. G. (2019). The effectiveness of quantitative easing: Evidence from Japan. *Journal of International Money and Finance, 99*, 102068.

Mian, A., & Sufi, A. (2009). The consequences of mortgage credit expansion: Evidence from the U.S. mortgage default crisis. *Quarterly Journal of Economics, 124*(4), 1449–1496.

Mishkin, F. S., & Posen, A. (1998). *Inflation targeting: Lessons from four countries*. NBER Working Paper.

Nakamura, E., & Steinsson, J. (2018). High-frequency identification of monetary non-neutrality: The information effect. *Quarterly Journal of Economics, 133*(3), 1283–1330.

Obstfeld, M. (2012). Financial flows, financial crises, and global imbalances. *Journal of International Money and Finance, 31*(3), 469–480.

Obstfeld, M., & Rogoff, K. (2009). *Global imbalances and the financial crisis: Products of common causes*. Working Paper.

Oosterloo, S., & De Haan, J. (2004). Central banks and financial stability: A survey. *Journal of Financial Stability, 1*(2), 257–273.

Romer, C. D., & Romer, D. H. (1998). *Monetary policy and the well-being of the poor* (NBER Working Paper No. 6793). National Bureau of Economic Research.

Romer, C. D., & Romer, D. H. (2000). Federal Reserve information and the behaviour of interest rates. *American Economic Review, 90*(3), 429–457.

Romer, C. D., & Romer, D. H. (2004). A new measure of monetary shocks: Derivation and implications. *American Economic Review, 94*(4), 1055–1084.

Romer, C. D., & Romer, D. H. (2023). Presidential address: Does monetary policy matter? The narrative approach after 35 years. *American Economic Review, 113*(6), 1395–1423.

Rudebusch, G. D. (2010). Macro-finance models of interest rates and the economy. *The Manchester School, 78*(s1), 25–52.

Runkel, C. N. (2022). European Central Bank: Term refinancing operations. *Journal of Financial Crises, 4*(2), 817–843.

Stevenson, B. (2020). The initial impact of COVID-19 on labor market outcomes across groups and the potential for permanent scarring. *The Hamilton Project, 16*, 1–11.

Svensson, L. E. (1997). Inflation forecast targeting: Implementing and monitoring inflation targets. *European Economic Review, 41*(1), 1111–1146.

Svensson, L. E. (2003). What is wrong with the Taylor rules? Using judgment in monetary policy through targeting rules. *Journal of Economic Literature, 41*(2), 426–477.

Svensson, L. E. (2010). Inflation targeting. In B. M. Friedman & M. Woodford (Eds.), *Handbook of monetary economics* (Vol. 3, pp. 1237–1302). Elsevier.

Svensson, L. E. (2012). Evaluating monetary policy. In E. F. Koening, R. Leeson, & G. A. Kahn (Eds.), *The Taylor rule and the transformation of monetary policy* (pp. 245–274). Hoover Institution Press.

Svensson, L. E. O. (2020). What rule for the Federal Reserve? Forecast targeting. *International Journal of Central Banking, 16*(6), 39–95.

Van Doornik, B., Igan, D., & Kharroubi, E. (2023). Labour markets: What explains the resilience. *BIS Quarterly Review, 77*.

Veronesi, P., & Zingales, L. (2010). Paulson's gift. *Journal of Financial Economics, 97*(3), 339–368.

Chapter 3
The Disclosure of Monetary Policy to the Public

3.1 Introduction

Although disclosure is usually a term that economists and practitioners attribute to the accounting literature, in recent years it has often been applied to discuss the progress in the communication strategy of central banks towards the public. As mentioned in the previous chapter, central banks implementing conventional or unconventional monetary policy, engaging with an innovative tool, or (and) promoting an innovative process or committee, are incomplete "moves" until the public is aware of it. Academic research has, in time, found empirical evidence that financial market participants are as likely to react to the disclosure and communication. In this chapter, we discuss the evolution of the communication and how the disclosure is carried out by the policymakers of three major central banks: the Federal Reserve, the European Central Bank, and the Bank of England.

Despite differences in timings and economic conditions, during the past three decades, these policymakers went through similar stages to enhance the public understanding of their actions, improving accountability, and, in the aftermath of the 2008 financial crisis, restoring credibility in the financial system. Across time, the policies changed along with the needs of the economy and the public, the mandates of central banks have evolved (and the process is not completed) to face the scenarios discussed in the first chapter. Central banks' communication has been part of this evolution, going from very little disclosure (in the '90 s) towards the recent use of social media and simplified language to reach households.

L. M. Murgia, *The Impact of Monetary Policy*, Financial and Monetary Policy Studies 56, https://doi.org/10.1007/978-3-032-15451-4_3

3.2 The Evolution of Central Banks Communication Policies

As mentioned in the first chapter, the advent of Inflation Targeting (IT) frameworks increased the accountability of policymakers. Most contemporary central banks' communication policies have evolved to accommodate the requirement for transparency and the need to managing the public expectations of the future path of macroeconomic variables as well as nominal interest rates. In this section, we discuss the evolution of central banks' communication, in relation to the events and macro scenario of the past three decades as well as the policymakers in charge of these decisions. It is important to keep in mind that how central banks disclose their information is part of the monetary policy toolkit per se (Blinder et al., 2024). Additionally, the financial crisis also stood for a major evolution in the central banks' communication, due to the need for policymakers to establish trust with the public (Blinder et al., 2017).

The way of approaching the general public has gone through considerable changes. The evolving approaches have been partially influenced by the evolution of social media and their related technologies. Blinder et al. (2024) report, using a sample of 75 banks, the different ways in which central banks outreach to the public. We report that evidence in Fig. 4.1, and as can be seen, most of the ways in which central banks currently engage with the public are related to social media, such as X (Twitter at the time) and YouTube.

3.2.1 The Federal Reserve and Its Chairs

In this subsection, we analyse the transformation that has accompanied the FED in the past three decades. We examine their way of disclosing their intentions and how their disclosure is not only necessary to create trust but is also effectively a monetary policy tool when conventional tools are unavailable.

We begin by delving into the basics of "how" the decisions are taken, and from whom. The Federal Open Market Committee (FOMC) is composed of 12 members, including the 7 members of the Board of Governors of the Federal Reserve System, the president of the Federal Reserve Bank of New York, and 4 of the remaining 11 Reserve Bank Presidents. Policy decisions are taken under a majority rule during FOMC meetings. The FOMC meets 8 times per year in pre-scheduled meetings and more rarely in conference calls, usually employed in emergency or crisis situations. The IT framework, discussed in the previous chapter, represented for most central banks the "cut-off" time for increasing transparency and accountability. However, the FED started this process before that, and its first step was to "pre-schedule" the meetings.

Furthermore, when the FED decided to "pre-schedule" the meetings, it did so by undertaking two major communication innovations. The first are the "Transcripts", introduced just after the pre-scheduling policy in 1994, and the "Minutes" that were started in 1993. That decision was taken under the leadership of Chair Alan Greenspan and the political support of President Clinton, who had little interest in criticizing the FOMC given the state of the economy (Todd, 2016). Transparency has characterized most of Chair Greenspan's time, particularly the second one. He started his role in the 1980s and ended it when he left the place to Ben Bernanke in the early 2000s.

The communication by Chair Greenspan was emblematic and worth investigating for several reasons. Greenspan's leadership was often both praised and questioned during different stages of the economic cycle in his terms. Bligh and Hess (2007) carried out a complex content analysis of Greenspan's FOMC press releases, announcements, and speeches. During economic downturns, Greenspan showed how relevant the current situation was, by emphasizing the present tense and losing "certainty" in his language. Conversely, during times of economic growth, his language indicated a stronger sense of certainty. What they conclude is that Greenspan was an excellent example of a pragmatic leader, given his "problem-focused", analytical, and problem-solving attitude. This communication strategy suggests to "followers" that the leader is strongly aware of the situation and invested in the situation (Bligh & Hess, 2007).

The successes of his leadership are well documented in Mishkin (2005)'s seminal work. Mishkin (2005) makes a comprehensive review of the FED activity under Greenspan, indicating the following elements as the main achievements:

"A strong implicit Nominal Anchor". This concept refers to tying down inflation expectations.

"A Forward-Looking Monetary Policy". Starting from the fact that monetary policy affects the economy with some delay, it is imperative that actions are taken prior to inflationary or deflationary events.

"Increasing Transparency". This point is related to what was previously discussed about the communication actions taken by the FED during Greenspan's terms.

The resulting effects were a higher credibility and trust in the FED as well as the flexibility of monetary policy rules. The work of Mishkin (2005) only places transparency in third place; however, the three elements are all directly connected by the increased public communication of the FED. The nominal anchor of inflation expectations was, in fact, effective in conjunction with the declaration of it.

Several opinions were formulated on the ability of Greenspan to communicate. For example, Jansen (2011) compares the clarity of communication between Volcker and Greenspan and suggests that the latter was "mumbling with great incoherence", as suggested by himself. Based on a readability scoring, Greenspan was less understandable than Volcker. The readability scoring is constructed on the number of words per sentences and syllables per words. Nonetheless, Greenspan was, according to research findings, the most influential communicator of his time, compared to all of his FOMC colleagues (Ehrmann & Fratzscher, 2007).

At this point, it is worth recalling, alongside the chairs, the innovations in terms of documents and information released to the public. A summary of all the old and new documents released and archived by the FED can be found in Table 3.1. As pointed out, under Greenspan, a major "transparency revolution" started,

Table 3.1 Documents published by the FED

Document name	Content description	Time frame
Transcripts	Detailed record of FOMC meetings proceedings	(1994–present)
Agendas	List of items to be covered at each FOMC meetings. To be received by the FOMC members a week before the meeting and released to the public together with the transcript	(since forever-present)
Policy statements	FOMC's public statements regarding its policy decisions	
Summary of economic projections	Compilation of FOMC participants' economic projections. FOMC meeting participants—The 7 members of the Board of Governors and the 12 presidents of the Federal Reserve Banks, all of whom participate in the deliberations of the FOMC—Submit individual economic projections in conjunction with four FOMC meetings a year. Beginning in December 2020, all SEP exhibits—which had previously been released three weeks after the meeting as an addendum to the minutes—are released in conjunction with the Chair's press conference. The written portion of the SEP was discontinued.	30/10/2007–present
Tealbooks	Economic analysis and description of policy alternatives. Tealbook A and B, merged from the green book and the blue book. Tealbook A: Economic and financial conditions: Current situation and outlook, produced by the staff of the Board of Governors. Tealbook B, officially subtitled "monetary policy: Strategies and alternatives", is produced by the staff of the Board of Governors to provide background and context on monetary policy alternatives that the FOMC could consider at a particular meeting. Tealbook B includes the same information that had been included in the bluebook, except that the financial developments content was moved to Tealbook A.	(2010–present)
Statement on Longer-Run Goals and Monetary Policy Strategy	This statement articulates the framework for monetary policy and serves as the foundation for the committee's policy actions	(2012–present)
Minutes	Summary of issues addressed at each FOMC meeting	(1993–present)
Greenbooks	Staff analysis of the US and international economy	(1964–2010)
Memoranda of discussions	Detailed account of discussions at FOMC meetings	(1967–1976)
Record of Policy Actions & Minutes actions	Precursor of the modern minutes.	(1964–2010)
Historical minutes	Records of discussions and decisions at FOMC meetings	(1936–1967)

(continued)

Table 3.1 (continued)

Document name	Content description	Time frame
Bluebooks	Background and context on monetary policy alternatives	(1965–2010)
Redbooks	Qualitative view of economic developments by districts	(1970–1983)

Source: FOMC historical material on federalreserve.gov

complementary to the advent of the popularity of Inflation targeting frameworks. The "transcripts" and the "minutes" also started to be published alongside the "Agendas" and the "Greenbooks". The Greenbooks, that were discontinued during Bernanke's terms, included the staff analysis of the domestic and international economy. These documents are worth mentioning, as they will be the extensive subject of discussion and research not only in the field of central banks communication strategies, but also in the field of monetary policy impact on the economy that will be discussed later in Chaps. 4 and 6.

The Greenbook, now called "Tealbook", complements the "Summary of Economic Projections", introduced in 2007, in providing a clear overview of the forecasts of the economy. Why is it particularly relevant? And how are these two documents different? While the Tealbook today (and the Greenbook before) includes the information related to the Survey of Professional Forecasters (SPF), the Summary of Economic Projections (SEP) document includes the view of the FOMC members on their expectations for the economy. The SPF is a quarterly survey of macroeconomic forecasts in the US, which began in 1968, conducted by the Federal Reserve Bank of Philadelphia and the National Bureau of Economic Research (NBER). The panellists are professional forecasters, with longstanding track records of macroeconomic forecasting.

To put it simple, the SPF is a professional external opinion given to the members of the FOMC, while the SEP is then the subsequent FOMC opinion. These two documents are complementary in supporting the public in anticipating the decisions of the FOMC. Anticipating or predicting the decision of the FOMC has been defined as a point of success of the communication strategy of central banks (Ehrmann & Fratzscher, 2007), particularly in supporting the broader strategy when conventional monetary tools were unavailable. This last point was particularly relevant in the aftermath of the financial crisis, when Bernanke was the FED Chair.

According to Blinder et al. (2008), the FOMC became very collegial in taking its decisions and communicating them under the leadership of Ben Bernanke, who succeeded Greenspan. Bernanke was a strong supporter of central bank communication as a tool, especially in increasing the commitment and accountability of the institution (Bernanke & Reinhart, 2004). Bernanke (2013) asserts that when he started his term, one of his priorities was to make the FED more transparent and the communication of monetary policy as accessible as possible. In his speech in 2013, he addresses several aspects of the evolution of the FED communication and how this was even more relevant after the financial crisis.

The discussion of transparency and accountability initiated with Greenspan was continued and expanded in the direction of influencing the public expectations.

Bernanke (2013) emphasized the importance of managing these expectations, which is done through clarifying the objectives of monetary policy. It is useful to recall that Bernanke during his term faced the 2008 financial crisis and the need for strong responses from institutions (as discussed in the previous chapter). The zero-lower bound limit posed a challenge that could have been mastered solely by managing expectations and "forward-guiding" them. This forward guidance had important effects on the FED's reaction function and on managing market participant expectations towards a "long-term" accommodative policy approach (Femia et al., 2013).

In a 2007 speech before the 25th Annual Monetary conference[1] Bernanke advocated again the necessity of transparency, as:

> Good communications are prerequisite if central banks are to maintain the democratic legitimacy and independence that are essential to sound monetary policy making.

This sentence is emblematic of the transformation that was happening worldwide on how central banks communicate with the public, because of the three elements included: legitimacy in democracy, independence and effectiveness in controlling monetary policy. Bernanke acknowledges the public role of central bankers and the need for them to provide explanations of their actions, which ultimately affect every citizen, through their elected representatives. This legitimizes the work of central banks and their operations and indirectly ensures their independence from the ongoing politics. Independence is necessary for several reasons, mainly to ensure effectiveness in the fight against inflation. Again, the discussion on inflation targeting and how this framework wouldn't work without the support of effective communication is indirectly remarked in the words of Bernanke. The last element is a "sound monetary policy". It is objectively hard to define a "sound" monetary policy strategy beforehand, given the endogeneity that arises among monetary policy tools and macroeconomic variables. However, the inflation targeting framework and central banks' mandate offered a goal for policymakers, an anchor for expectations, and an objective measure of performance evaluation.

The evolution of central banks' communication started just prior to the 2008 financial crisis. In a speech on the economic outlook at the US Congress, Bernanke gave extremely detailed explanations on the steps taken by the FED in 2007 given the recent developments in the housing market and the initial financial turmoil created by the contrasting views of the quality of subprime mortgages.

During Bernanke's term, international financial stability and how to avoid domino effects became the centre of the discussion. This was highlighted in a speech given at the New York Economic Club during the bursting period of the financial crisis (October 2008), where he clearly stated that help to private-sector institutions should only be given when international financial stability is at risk. Once again, in this speech, Bernanke was extremely clear about the FED's position and opinion on the state of the economy as well as on the government's actions.

[1] https://www.federalreserve.gov/newsevents/speech/bernanke20071114a.htm

The aftermath of the financial crisis increased the need for greater transparency not only of the FED's actions, but also of the state of the economy. The sudden nature of the breakout of the financial crisis, and the speed at which it propagated around the world, alarmed investors, who increasingly sought to forecast the broad macroeconomic variables and the actions of the FED. The discussion on financial stability became imperative, as policymakers realized the importance of financial markets as a monetary policy conduit (Barsistha & Kurov, 2008). To this end, in the 2012 document "Statement on Longer-Run Goals and Monetary Policy Strategy", the foundation for the actions of the FED was created and circulated. That document highlighted the long run goals and the objectives of the FED, reinforcing the "forward guidance" concept stressed by Bernanke and increasing the accountability of the FED for the long-run goals.

The role played by financial markets in the transmission mechanism of monetary policy and how they are inevitably affected by it will be further discussed in this book. What is relevant to the purpose of the discussion on communication is how the public started to perceive that institutions and policymakers were preferring the wealth of investors over the wellbeing of the public. In this context, Janet Yellen was particularly vocal in highlighting that the FED works "through" financial markets and not "for" them. In her famous 2014 speech, right at the start of her mandate, she remarked that the goal of the FED was to "help Main Street, not Wall Street".[2]

The term of Janet Yellen was characterized by less "innovations" in terms of the documents produced by the FOMC and disclosed to the public. However, Janet Yellen continued the campaign of Bernanke's credibility and accountability of the FED. As per Bernanke's approach, Janet Yellen also was very involved in academic research on monetary policy and central banks' communication. For example, in her study "Enhancing FED Credibility" (Yellen, 2006), she discusses and reiterates the importance of the inflation anchor to manage public expectations and how this is an effective tool to manage monetary policy.

When Janet Yellen was nominated by President Obama, it didn't surprise the public, not only because her main competitor (Larry Summers) withdrew his name, but also because her leadership style was in line with the current economic conditions. Her abilities in forecasting the economy were well known, along with the clarity of her communication style, an essential element during the continuation of the zero-lower bound period.

In a speech that she gave at the "Society of American Business Editors and Writers 50th Anniversary Conference"[3] she provided a comparison on how the communications of central banks affect monetary policy. We wish to reiterate it, as it provides the clearest example of why communication, together with the tools, is an essential component of the transmission mechanism of monetary policy. In the speech, she highlights that if we were talking about transportation policies and a new road project was announced, the benefits for the public will only arise at the end

[2] https://www.federalreserve.gov/newsevents/speech/yellen20140331a.htm

[3] https://www.federalreserve.gov/newsevents/speech/yellen20130404a.htm

of the project, regardless of how it is communicated to the public. Monetary policy works differently. The effects of monetary policy are, in fact, strongly dependent, as demonstrated by a large body of research, on public expectations.

Having mainly described the communication strategies of three very influential chairs of the FED, it is worth recalling that we have mainly focused on the content released and the leadership skills of these three past FED chairs. Recently, and given new available machine learning tools, the attention has been moved not only to *what* they say, but to *how* they say it. A recent work from Alexopoulos et al. (2024) focuses on their voice and facial expressions to identify the markets' reaction to how they express themselves. The research is focused on Bernanke and Yellen and finds compelling evidence that the limitations posed by the content that they can potentially release can be surmounted in the way they say it.

The three discussed chairs therefore had the difficult task of transforming the communication of the FED throughout different business cycles and unprecedented times. Perhaps the last chair, however, had the even more arduous task to bring it forward during the pandemic, the most unprecedented and unexpected of the crises. The breakout of the pandemic tested the communication abilities of many government leaders and policymakers, with many of them unfortunately not being up to the task. Even worse, if during normal market times investors and the public might display "limited attention" due to the amount of information that normally hits the market on an ordinary trading day, during the pandemic eyes and ears were fully focused on institutional announcements.

The very recent work of Narain and Sangani (2023) offers very valuable insights into the comparison among the press releases of the last three mentioned chairs, Bernanke, Yellen, and the current Powell. Although the importance of the press releases in the context of the public reaction was already established (Boguth et al., 2019), less work is yet available on Jerome Powell and the pandemic. What they find, which is in line with the heightened attention of the public, is that since the start of the pandemic the press conferences are responsible for heightened market volatility and tend to move in the opposite direction compared to the FOMC statement. During the Bernanke and Yellen period, it was exactly the opposite; their communication tends to, in fact, reinforce the FOMC statement.

In Fig. 1 of Narain and Sangani (2023), they plot the average volatility during Yellen's press conferences (blue line) and Powell's press conferences (red line). Squared market returns (proxy for high-frequency volatility) are three times higher in Powell than in the rest of the chairs. It is worth noting that the unexpected press releases in March 2020 are excluded from their sample. They also report empirical evidence of reversal effects in market returns after Powell's conferences, which is in contrast with the previous findings of Boguth et al. (2019).

3.2.2 *The European Central Bank and Its Presidents*

The evolution of the European Central Bank's (ECB) communication channels reflects both the changing landscape of monetary policy and the personal imprint of each of its four presidents. From its founding in 1998 under Wim Duisenberg through the eras of Jean-Claude Trichet, Mario Draghi, and Christine Lagarde, the ECB has progressively broadened its toolkit. The presidents moved from a specialist-only communication to a technical discourse, a multi-layered strategy, and ultimately something more in line with the understanding of the general public. Each president has brought in a specific innovation in terms of transparency, clarity, and outreach.

When Wim Duisenberg took office in June 1998, the ECB faced the immediate challenge of establishing credibility for Europe's new single currency. From the outset, the Governing Council settled on a fixed schedule of six-weekly press conferences following monetary policy decisions—an approach more systematic than that of most peers at the time. These conferences comprised an "introductory statement" in English, immediately published on the ECB website, followed by a live Q&A in multiple languages. The ECB also launched its Monthly Bulletin, targeted at academics and market analysts, and published staff macroeconomic projections for the euro area for the first time in June 2001. Under Duisenberg's low-key style, the emphasis was on reliability and procedural clarity, laying the groundwork for future enhancements in transparency and accountability.

Jean-Claude Trichet's presidency brought a marked intensification in both frequency and diversity of channels. In November 2004, the ECB began publishing point forecasts alongside projection ranges, and in June 2005 expanded the projections to include quarterly profiles and detailed narrative boxes, improving interpretability for markets. Trichet also championed what has come to be known as the "Account of the Monetary Policy Meetings" (first published in 2007), summarizing the Governing Council's economic and monetary analysis in plain language. Moreover, he shifted press conferences from morning to early afternoon to accommodate wider media participation and encouraged Executive Board members to give speeches and interviews across euro-area capitals, thereby broadening the ECB's audience beyond financial markets. Empirical studies show that under Trichet the length and clarity of introductory statements increased, as did the breadth of topics covered in Q&A sessions, helping to anchor market expectations more firmly (Ehrmann & Fratzscher, 2009a, 2009b; Pavelkova, 2022; Klejdysza & Lumsdaine, 2023).

Mario Draghi's tenure coincided with unprecedented crises, and his communication style became a policy tool. In July 2012, his now-famous "whatever it takes" pledge exemplified the power of off-script remarks to restore confidence. Building on Trichet's meeting accounts, in June 2015 the ECB introduced fully fledged "Monetary Policy Accounts", offering comprehensive transcripts of internal debate for the first time. Draghi also pioneered the use of conditional forward guidance, which required more detailed explanations and thus enriched press-conference content (Klejdysza & Lumsdaine, 2023). On the digital front, the ECB revamped its website in 2014 to host multimedia material, webcasts of press conferences, infographics, and podcasts, with the intention of making communication more accessible to non-specialists.

Christine Lagarde's arrival marked a further broadening in scope and tone. As part of the ECB's 2021 monetary policy strategy review, she committed to "listen more" and to integrate climate change analysis into policy communication. Under her leadership, the ECB launched "ECB Explains", a video-and-blog series aimed at demystifying monetary policy for the general public and significantly expanded its social-media footprint on Twitter, LinkedIn, and YouTube. Recognizing that speeches by Executive Board members vary in clarity, Lagarde encouraged simpler language, a move confirmed by recent readability analyses showing a marked drop in the education level needed to understand ECB talks during her tenure (Bjerkander & Glas, 2024). She also introduced "ECB Listens" public-engagement webinars, where citizens can pose questions directly to Governing Council members, further democratizing policy dialogue.

3.2.3 *Bank of England and Its Governors*

This subsection outlines how the Bank of England's communication strategy has evolved under each Governor, from the pre-independence period through to the present day, highlighting key innovations in transparency, clarity, and outreach. Before formal independence in 1997, the BOE set interest rates on advice from the Chancellor of the Exchequer, and communications were tightly controlled by Treasury briefings. The communications were very limited, and the public statements of the Governor were rare and very technical. Additionally, as also discussed in the previous chapter, the numerical target of inflation was not set. Sir Edward "Eddie" George, who served between 1993 and 2003, laid the groundwork for openness. The operational independence of the BOE was granted by the Parliament in 1997. The BOE was now formally autonomous in setting the Bank Rate and the Monetary Policy Committee (MPC) was rigorously following the numerical target of inflation set around 2%.

To further foster accountability, the BOE launched the Inflation Report (IR) in 1997, containing the forecasts for inflation and growth. The document provided evidence of the information set available to policymakers and enabled the public to directly link their actions to their economic expectations. The commentary that came alongside the numerical forecasts offered also a first example of forward guidance by the BOE. The early issues of the IR were still highly technical and mainly intended for financial market participants, afterwards the language and message were simplified. The IR is now a document that is highly used and commented on also by the academic community. The IR could be easily compared to the FED Greenbook, discussed previously, and analogously highly employed in research pieces that will be further discussed in Chaps. 4 and 5.

May and June 1999 experienced a lot of innovation in the communication strategy and documents of the BOE. First, in May 1999, half-annual press conferences were instituted. And further in June 1999, BOE began publishing MPC minutes and individual voting records. According to research, the publishing of the minutes and voting records supports the reduction of market uncertainty about future interest rates and lowers the volatility of the term structure of interest rates. Benford et al.

(2009) discuss this in the specific case of the BOE and its quantitative easing programs.

Transparency and narrative clarity were definitely improved under the guidance of Sir Mervyn King, who served as BOE governor between 2003 and 2013. The frequency of the press conferences increased to a monthly rhythm in 2003, pairing a policy statement with a live session of Q&As. Ehrmann et al. (2008) find that this step sharply improved private-sector anchoring of expectations. Under King, the IR adopted "fan charts" in February 2007, graphically depicting uncertainty around projections. This innovation made risks transparent and allowed the BOE to communicate not just central forecasts but alternative scenarios. King's communication ability was praised during the 2008 financial crisis as he used ad hoc speeches to explain emergency measures.

In August 2013, Carney introduced explicit "thresholds" for guidance: policy rates would stay at record lows until unemployment fell below 7% (subject to inflation risks). Tenreyro and Thwaites (2016) show that attaching such conditions to rate guidance significantly improved its effectiveness in shaping medium-term yields. When inflation deviated more than 1 percentage point from target, Carney wrote public letters to the Chancellor explaining the variance. This novel "one-for-one" mechanism deepened accountability and is credited with strengthening the BOE's credibility. Recognizing changing media habits, Carney's team began webcasting press conferences in 2013 and launched the BOE's first Twitter feed for real-time policy updates. Joyce et al. (2011) note that the use of these channels broadened reach beyond traditional financial market audiences. In 2015 the BOE rolled out an online dashboard allowing users to build custom charts from historical data. The initiative was praised for democratizing access to central bank statistics.

Andrew Bailey brought forward the idea of inclusivity, attention to the climate crisis, and the general engagement with the public. In 2021 Bailey inaugurated quarterly "Listening Events", where citizens pose questions directly to MPC members. These are webcast and archived, echoing the ECB's "Listens" webinars and aiming to bring non-expert views into policy debates. Bailey's BOE integrated climate-risk analysis into its regular Financial Stability Reports (2021 onward), supplementing technical annexes with plain-language summaries. A 2022 study by Broadbent and Haldane (2023) documents a marked reduction in the complexity of MPC minutes and press-conference transcripts under Bailey, lowering the Flesch-Kincaid reading score by two grade levels.

3.3 New Developments of the Communication Strategy

Having discussed the evolution of the communication strategies of the major central banks, it is worth now spending a few words on what the future developments could be. First, who will be the ultimate receiver of the communications, and second what would be the new content. As mentioned, in the words of policymakers and central bankers, the public is the ultimate receiver of the communications and the policy effects. The issue with the public is obviously the language and content complexity.

The issue of communicating complex financial concepts to the public was prominent in the aftermath of the financial crisis, since it was clear that individuals had little understanding of the financial products and dynamics. The worldwide regulation has extensively advanced in that respect, to ensure that the required level of financial literacy for the understanding of investment products was relatively low. Financial literacy and inclusion are of great interest to policymakers, such as the Financial Conduct Authority (FCA) in the UK,[4] which are partially aligned with why central bankers have great interest in being understandable to the public. As discussed in the previous chapter, the economic behaviour of agents and expectations need to be influenced, obviously this becomes much more effective when a bigger chunk of the population is involved and not only investors and practitioners. Second, the advent of new unregulated investment opportunities, such as cryptocurrencies, has made imperative the need for the general population to enhance their understanding of concepts such as savings and risk. Why should this concern both central bankers and financial market authorities? A number of reasons, spanning from the fact that cryptocurrencies might undermine the monetary sovereignty of central banks as well as the financial stability if a large portion of the population is subject to their volatility swings by owning them.

Cryptocurrencies, fiat currency, and central bank digital currencies are the new topics of discussion, which are even more directly related to the public interest. For example, the Digital Euro (DE), proposed and developed by the ECB, will soon be available to the public, giving everyone the chance to own a money account directly with a central bank. Cardillo et al. (2024) discuss the implications for the cryptocurrency market of central bank communication on the DE arrival, by collecting a novel sample of press-releases, interviews, and announcements. Ultimately, research should focus on the implications for households and their savings (or consumption) attitudes, of central banks' communication.

References

Alexopoulos, M., Han, X., Kryvtos, O., & Zhang, X. (2024). More than words: Fed chairs' communication during congressional testimonies. *Journal of Monetary Economics, 142*, 1–17.

Bailey, A. (2021, November). *The Bank's climate change roadmap*. Bank of England Speech.

Barsistha, A., & Kurov, A. (2008). Macroeconomic cycles and the stock market's reaction to monetary policy. *Journal of Banking & Finance, 32*(2), 2606–2616.

Bean, C. (2009). Monetary policy after the fall. *Revue d'économie financière, 96*(1), 15–26.

Benford, J., Berry, S., Nikolov, K., Psaradakis, Z., & Wright, S. (2009). Nowcasting inflation. *Bank of England Quarterly Bulletin, Q1*, 36–46.

Bernanke, B. S. (2003). A perspective on inflation targeting. *Business Economics*, 7–15.

Bernanke, B. S. (2004). *The great moderation*. Federal Reserve Board Speech.

[4] https://word-edit.officeapps.live.com/we/wordeditorframe.aspx?WOPISrc=https://wopi.dropbox.com/wopi/files/oid_5116089298216921088&cloud_editor=word&dl=0&ui=it#_ftn6

Bernanke, B. (2013). *Communication and monetary policy*. Speech at the National Economists Club Dinner.

Bernanke, B. S., & Mishkin, F. S. (1997). Inflation targeting: A new framework for monetary policy? *Journal of Economic Perspectives, 11*(2), 97–116.

Bernanke, B., & Reinhart, V. R. (2004). Conducting monetary policy at very low short-term interest rates. *American Economic Review, 94*(2), 85–90.

Bjerkander, L., & Glas, A. (2024). Talking in a language that everyone can understand? Clarity of speeches by the ECB Executive Board. *Journal of International Money and Finance, 149*, 103200.

Bligh, M. C., & Hess, G. D. (2007). The power of leading subtly: Alan Greenspan, rhetorical leadership, and monetary policy. *The Leadership Quarterly, 18*(1), 87–104.

Blinder, A. S., & Morgan, J. (2005). Are two heads better than one? Monetary policy by committee. *Journal of Money, Credit and Banking, 37*(5), 789–811.

Blinder, A. S., Ehrmann, M., Fratzscher, M., de Haan, J., & Jansen, D.-J. (2008). Central bank communication and monetary policy: A survey of theory and evidence. *Journal of Economic Literature, 46*(4), 910–945.

Blinder, A. S., Ehrmann, M., de Haan, J., & Jansen, D.-J. (2017). Necessity as the mother of invention: Monetary policy after crisis. *Economic Policy, 92*(1), 707–755.

Blinder, A. S., Ehrmann, M., De Haan, J., & Jansen, D.-J. (2024). Central bank communication with the general public: Promise or false hope? *Journal of Economic Literature, 62*(2), 425–457.

Boguth, O., Grégoire, V., & Martineau, C. (2019). Shaping expectations and coordinating attention: The unintended consequences of FOMC press conferences. *Journal of Financial and Quantitative Analysis, 54*(6), 2327–2353.

Broadbent, B., & Haldane, A. (2023). Democratizing monetary policy: Public webinars at the Bank of England. *Oxford Economic Papers, 75*(2), 457–476.

Cardillo, G., Monaco, E., & Murgia, L. M. (2024). A *Battle for sovereignty: Crypto market response to CBDC informational spillover*. Available at SSRN 4906873.

Carney, M. (2014). One-for-one letters: Strengthening accountability. *Bank of England Quarterly Bulletin, Q2*, 121–130.

Ehrmann, M., & Fratzscher, M. (2007). Communication by central bank committee members: Different strategies, same effectiveness? *Journal of Money, Credit and Banking, 39*(2–3), 509–540.

Ehrmann, M., & Fratzscher, M. (2009a). Explaining monetary policy in press conferences. *International Journal of Central Banking, 5*(2), 41–84.

Ehrmann, M., & Fratzscher, M. (2009b). Explaining monetary policy in press conferences: The experience of the European Central Bank. *International Journal of Central Banking, 5*(2), 43–73.

Ehrmann, M., & Wabitsch, A. (2021). *Central bank communication with non-experts: A road to nowhere? ECB* Working Paper Series No. 2594.

Ehrmann, M., Fratzscher, M., de Haan, J., & Jansen, D.-J. (2008). Communicating central bank decisions: The communication tools of the ECB and the Fed. *Journal of Monetary Economics, 55*(6), 983–999.

European Central Bank. (2021). *ECB monetary policy communication in a changing world* (Occasional Paper Series No. 274).

Femia, K., Friedman, S., & Sack, B. (2013). *The effects of policy guidance on perceptions of the Fed's reaction function*. Staff Report, Federal Reserve Bank of New York.

Filardo, A., & Guinigundo, D. (2008). *Transparency and communication in monetary policy: A survey of Asian central banks*. Bank for International Settlements.

Geraats, P. M. (2006). Transparency of monetary policy: Theory and practice. *CESifo Economic Studies, 52*(1), 111–152.

Glas, A., & Müller, L. (2023). *Talking in a language that everyone can understand? Clarity of speeches by the ECB Executive Board*. Discussion Paper No. 23-073, University of Mannheim.

Goodhart, C., & Lim, G. C. (2009). Central bank communication: Speakers and listeners. *Oxford Review of Economic Policy, 25*(4), 475–495.
Haan, J., & Jansen, D.-J. (2024). Central Bank Communication with the General Public: Promise or False Hope? *Journal of Economic Literature, 62*(2), 425–457.
Ito, T., & Mishkin, F. S. (2004). Two decades of Japanese monetary policy and the deflation problem. In B. S. Bernanke & M. Woodford (Eds.), *NBER international seminar on macroeconomics* (pp. 91–146). Cambridge University Press.
Jansen, D.-J. (2011). Mumbling with great incoherence: Was it really so difficult to understand Alan Greenspan? *Economics Letters, 113*(1), 70–72.
Joyce, M., Lasaosa, A., Stevens, I., & Tong, M. (2011). The financial market impact of quantitative easing in the United Kingdom. *International Journal of Central Banking, 7*(3), 113–161.
King, M. (2009, November). *Twenty years of inflation targeting*. Speech at the Center for Monetary and Financial Studies, Madrid.
Klejdysza, J., & Lumsdaine, R. L. (2023). Shifts in ECB communication: A textual analysis of the press conferences. *International Journal of Central Banking, 19*(2), 473–542.
McLeay, M., Radia, A., & Thomas, R. (2014). Money in the modern economy: An introduction. *Bank of England Quarterly Bulletin, Q1*, 4–13.
Mishkin, F. S. (2005). The Fed after Greenspan. *Eastern Economic Journal, 31*(3), 317–332.
Mishkin, F. S., & Posen, A. S. (1997). *Inflation targeting: Lessons from four countries*. NBER Working Paper, 1–135.
Narain, N., & Sangani, K. (2023). *The market impact of Fed communications: The role of the press conference*. Available at SSRN 4354333.
Oshima, Y., & Matsubayashi, Y. (2018). *Monetary policy communication of the Bank of Japan: Computational text analysis*. (Discussion Paper No. 1816). Graduate School of Economics, Kobe University.
Pavelkova, A. (2022). *The ECB press conference: A textual analysis* (ECB Working Paper No. 2742). European Central Bank.
Shibamoto, M. (2016). *Empirical assessment of the impact of monetary policy communication on the financial market (DP2016-19)*. Research Institute for Economics & Business Administration, Kobe University.
Tenreyro, S., & Thwaites, G. (2016). PDE experiments at the Bank of England: Forward guidance and its impacts. *Journal of Monetary Economics, 84*, 108–126.
Tetlock, P. C. (2014). Information transmission in finance. *Annual Review of Financial Economics, 6*(1), 365–384.
Todd, T. (2016). *A corollary of accountability: A history of the FOMC policy communication*. Working Paper, Federal Reserve Bank of Kansas City, 1–40.
Yellen, J. L. (2006). Enhancing Fed credibility. *Business Economics, 41*(1), 7–13.

Chapter 4
The Effects of the Disclosure to Financial Markets: Monetary Policy Announcements, Surprises, and Asset Pricing

4.1 Introduction

What happens when policymakers disclose information on the economic outlook and the future path of monetary policy? To address the question, the next chapters will delve into the analysis of the consequences of central banker statements, and how monetary policy announcements propagate significant effects in the economy. This chapter will focus on the "unintended effects".

To start, it would be useful to recall past FED Chair Janet Yellen when in 2014 made the following remark:

> Although we work through financial markets, our goal is to help Main Street, not Wall Street.

Despite the obvious intention of undermining the public opinion that the Chairs of the FED were often supporting financial markets, in the end, Yellen statement is simply reinforcing the common wisdom that the FED is well aware that when they talk, they will be influencing financial markets. Financial markets are, in fact, a fundamental component when monetary policymaker discloses their views and decisions. However, when the transmission process starts, it goes through policymakers and central banker announcements and press releases, which are spread into various news outlets. Those announcements are carefully inspected and followed by expert opinions and interpretations.

The monetary policy" announcement effect" has become an interesting area of research, which is closely related to the disclosure and communication techniques discussed in the previous chapter. The evolution of technologies to communicate with markets has in fact evolved hand in hand with the evolution of investor behaviour and approaches when reading and interpreting economic and financial news. In this chapter we present an analysis of how investors react to public announcements, how their expectations shape this reaction, and the several ways in which the literature has attempted to investigate these phenomena.

L. M. Murgia, *The Impact of Monetary Policy*, Financial and Monetary Policy Studies 56, https://doi.org/10.1007/978-3-032-15451-4_4

We first acknowledge the influence of expectations and how the literature has evolved in developing methodologies to gauge these expectations and financial market reactions. Interestingly, this topic has extended to the industry and practitioners, who are very much interested in understanding "what the rest of the market thinks". Two different industry metrics are proposed and shown in the chapter, providing evidence of the strong link between research and practical knowledge, as well as validating the high impact of this research stream.

The next topic of this chapter is on financial market reactions to macroeconomic announcements, disclosed by policymakers with a specific emphasis on the Federal Open Market Committee announcement (FOMC), which has sparked an entire stream of literature. FOMC announcements are the highest rank and most anticipated public announcements. Around FOMC meetings and their subsequent announcements, a large percentage of the annual returns of the S&P500 are realized, surprisingly with limited risk. These findings are of interest to both the academia and the financial industry because of the difficulties in reconciling the empirical findings with predictions of standard asset pricing theoretical models.

The chapter shows these patterns and how they have changed throughout the business cycle and across different economic scenarios, such as the Global Financial crisis. Since most of the empirical evidence presented refers to a period prior to the COVID-19 pandemic, we include novel results of the reactions of financial markets to FOMC announcements in Table 4.1. The results show that the pandemic period presents, as expected, different dynamics compared to previous times. We offer this as a potential outlet and inspiration for future, much needed, research on the subject.

The chapter concludes with two highly debated field questions: (a) do FOMC announcements have "global relevance"? Recent empirical research shows that when the FOMC talks, these most anticipated announcements are the highest ranked not only in the US capital markets, but also across the global financial system; (b) Which theory explains that "international ruling"? The question has generated a prolonged discussion, however, there isn't yet a consensus.

4.2 Monetary Policy Surprises and Asset Pricing

When discussing monetary policy surprises, the first milestone research is the famous "Kuttner Surprise", developed by Kenneth Kuttner[1] in 2001. The aim of his work was very straightforward: he proposed to separate the expected from the unexpected component of a change in the Federal Funds Rate. The term "surprise" is, in fact, specifically referred to the unexpected component of the change in the level of interest rates. Being unexpected and not yet incorporated into the price system, it

[1] Kenneth N. Kuttner is a professor of economics at Williams College. Between 1997 and 2003 he was Assistant Vice President at the Federal Reserve Bank of New York. He was also the coordinator of "FOMC Briefing Topics" for the Domestic Research function. For more information, see his personal page.

Table 4.1 Post-pandemic data

Years	FOMC Meetings	Announcement Days		Non-Announcement Days	
		Average of SP500 Returns	St. Deviation of SP500 Returns	Average of SP500 Returns	St. Deviation of SP500 Returns
2020	8	0.25	0.49	0.03	0.93
2021	8	−0.08	0.14	0.04	0.36
2022	8	−0.05	0.51	−0.02	0.67
2023	8	0.19	0.36	0.03	0.35
2024	1	−0.03	/	0.03	0.23
Total	**33**	**0.07**	**0.41**	**0.02**	**0.62**
	FOMC meetings	**Average of Delta VIX**	**St. deviation of Delta VIX**	**Average of Delta VIX**	**St. deviation of Delta VIX**
2020	8	−1.23	2.42	0.07	3.54
2021	8	0.22	1.05	−0.03	2.09
2022	8	−0.61	1.83	−0.10	1.69
2023	8	−0.52	1.30	−0.04	0.96
2024	1	−0.29	/	0.05	0.44
Total	**33**	**−0.53**	**1.70**	**−0.02**	**2.26**

Note: The table presents the summary statistics for FOMC announcement days as well as non--announcement days since 2020 until now. Overall, there are 33 meetings included in the sample, 8 scheduled per year. We have excluded the non-scheduled meeting from 2020. We report the S&P500 average return and the standard deviation of the returns. Similarly, we provide summary statistics for changes in the VIX index

Source: Refinitiv Eikon and FOMC website (https://www.federalreserve.gov/monetarypolicy/fomccalendars.htm) data and author computations

should surprise markets and therefore cause asset prices to move significantly. At that time, the topic was of particular interest to both economists and practitioners. Naturally, bondholders were more concerned than others about how the FOMC announcement would be impacting their investments. As it is well known, an increase in market interest rates will lead to a sudden decrease in bond prices. Kuttner (2001)'s results are consistent with the expectation hypothesis, and he shows that there is a significant link between unanticipated changes and a spectrum of market interest rates.

His work has been the starting point of the now vast literature stream that examines financial markets' reaction around monetary policy changes. Earlier, Cook and Hahn (1989) attempted to regress the change in fixed income instruments (e.g., Treasury Bills and bond rates) on the change in the Federal Funds Rate. Their findings show a positive and statistically significant response at different maturities, including a lagged response on T-bills rates. Kuttner (2001) revised their work in his paper, showing that the coefficient magnitude of the response is significantly smaller in a sample period posterior to Cook and Hahn (1989)'s work.

Based on his findings, Kuttner (2001) postulated that interest rate changes could have been anticipated by market participants, with its price impact significantly reduced, and concluded that his results are consistent with expectations theory.

Kuttner has been a pioneer in developing the methodology to disentangle the expected from the unexpected component of interest rate changes by taking advantage of prices determined in the Federal Funds Futures market. That market and its price system are a natural market-based proxy for investor expectations. It is worth recalling that the FED futures contract market was established in 1989 at the Chicago Board of Trade. These market-based metrics were, in fact, not yet largely employed in the literature. In a preceding work with Krueger, Kuttner analyses their predictability power with respect to the changes in the Federal Funds Rates.

Kuttner (2001) postulated that the unexpected change is therefore computed as the daily difference of futures settlement prices around a Federal Fund Target Day change. The equation writes as follows:

$$\Delta \tilde{r}_t^u = \frac{m}{m-t}\left(f_{s,t}^0 - f_{s,t-1}\right) \tag{4.1}$$

where $m/(m-t)$ is a scalar to account for the number of trading days in a month and depends on when the day changed. When assessing the one-day response on different bond maturities, the magnitude of the unexpected component is considerably larger and statistically significant. It is worth noting that at the time Kuttner distinguished between changes that happened during a defined FOMC announcement and on non-announcement dates.

Kuttner (2001) work looked at the fixed income market, however, even more popular was the work, co-authored with past FED Chair Bernanke (Bernanke & Kuttner, 2005) that shed first light on the effect of monetary policy surprises on equity prices. Their paper discussed the instantaneous effects of monetary policy surprises on the economy (computed mostly by the use of high-frequency data), and was the first to show the impact on equity prices and highlight the first step of the monetary policy transmission channel. This aspect is emphasized in the first paragraph of their paper that points out the importance of understanding the relationship between monetary policy actions and asset pricing as the most immediate and direct effect that these actions have.

The conventional wisdom on the effects of monetary policy on financial markets was mainly focused on the changes in the value of private portfolios ("the wealth effect") and the changes in the cost of capital. Bernanke and Kuttner (2005) point out that equity markets are unlikely to respond to "anticipated" policy actions. Although they don't explicitly mention it, an implication of their statement is to validate the Efficient Market Hypothesis (e.g., Fama (1970)). In other words, stock prices would have already discounted possible changes in their cost of capital, if the change in monetary policy was expected. At proof of this statement are the results which are obtained with the same equation as in Kuttner (2001) to estimate monetary policy surprises (Equation 4.1). His results show that value-weighted equity prices roughly gain 1% on an announcement day of a 25 basis point easing surprise. But what explains this response? Bernanke and Kuttner (2005) suggest that in the absence of complete asset pricing model it is difficult to distinguish a theoretical explanation from a market overreaction. The theoretical explanation is related to the expectation of future excess equity returns, in other words, changes in the equity premium. Very few papers at the time, and not many more as of now, attempt to provide a complete explanation for this reaction.

To further reaffirm the importance of the breakthrough methodology proposed in Kuttner (2001) and Bernanke and Kuttner (2005), their research papers have respectively more than 2500 and 3500 citations.

Their studies represent, in fact, the basis for all the following literature on FOMC announcements, surprises, and asset pricing that will be further discussed in this chapter. The literature has explored different asset classes and their reaction to monetary policy surprises. Interestingly, the recent field research has been focusing on the advent of new assets, such as "Digital Assets".

Even though the latest studies are still at a very early stage of development, it is worth mentioning them as a possible unexplored research outlet for field scholars. Kyriazis et al. (2023) design their research strategy on the Bernanke and Kuttner (2005) methodology, and find that Bitcoin (BTC) and Ethereum (ETH) volatilities are affected by surprises around FOMC announcement days.

As discussed in Chap. 3, several measures of shocks and surprises were developed by relying on that methodology. Two research directions are typically adopted: (a) exploiting high-frequency data that reduce the time-window around central banks announcements (from days to minutes); (b) comparing price reactions across different asset classes.

4.2.1 Industry Measures Employing Federal Funds Futures

In 2007 the Chicago Mercantile Exchange Group (CME Group) was formed by the merger of the Chicago Mercantile and the Chicago Board of Trade (CBOT). A further Group consolidation added the New York Mercantile Exchange (NYMEX) and the Commodity Exchange Inc. (COMEX). The group is mainly known for providing a platform to trade many different financial products, from the early 70s launch of derivatives markets such as futures and options contracts.

The CME Group introduced a tool named the CME FedWatch tool, which employs historical and current data from the federal funds futures market to gauge the probability of an FOMC interest rate change. The CME FedWatch methodology[2] is built on a few reasonable assumptions and derives the implied Effective Federal Funds Rates (EFFR) by adjusting it with future prices. The implied EFFR is calculated at the beginning and at the end of the month when the FOMC announcement is scheduled. The difference between the two is the expected change, that can

[2] The complete methodology description and usage can be found at https://www.cmegroup.com/articles/2023/understanding-the-cme-group-fedwatch-tool-methodology.html

be broken down into FOMC actions, assuming that Federal Funds Target rates are always changed within the interval of ±25 basis points. These actions are then transformed into a probability that gives an instrument, easy to interpret, to the markets and to the public.

It is important to notice that given the high-frequency data employed in the methodology, probabilities can evolve on a daily and weekly basis.

The global leading provider of financial data, analytics, and news, Bloomberg, also includes a similar feature in its terminal. Bloomberg, in fact, has a specific "FOMC" function[3] that shows the FOMC meeting schedules per year (historical as well as forthcoming), a decision analysis and commentary, the statement release times (minutes and votes), as well as related news.

Additionally and very close to the resource provided by the CME Group is the Bloomberg "WIRP" function, which stands for World Interest Rates Probabilities. Similarly, this function provides an estimate of market expectations regarding the future of interest rates, including, but not limited to the FED, the ECB, and the BOE.

4.3 Macroeconomic Announcements and Asset Pricing

Monetary policy statements are part of a larger set of news disclosure commonly known as macroeconomic announcements. They usually come when markets are open for trading, at scheduled times, and convey a significant amount of information that practitioners give consideration to their stand in financial markets. FOMC announcements are a subset of these macroeconomic announcements. In this sect. I review the state of the art of the financial literature on this topic, that mostly focuses on how the announcements are made and their effect on asset pricing.

Macroeconomic announcements are pre-scheduled announcements to provide early notice to financial market participants. Several offices and national organizations (e.g., the Office for National Statistics in the UK or the Bureau of Labor Statistics in the US), release updated information on macroeconomic variables, such as inflation and unemployment. Clearly, different macroeconomic variables are updated at different frequencies, with monthly releases being the norm. For example, the US Bureau of Labor Statistics regularly discloses macroeconomic variables such as the Consumer Price Index (CPI), the unemployment rate, and recently payroll employment. Differently, in the UK, for example, the first streamed information are Employment, Unemployment, Inflation, and GDP.[4] These policies of unveiling key fundamental data point out that different countries will prioritize different macroeconomic variables to perform as economic leading indicators.

[3] For a primer on Bloomberg functions and its use see: https://data.bloomberglp.com/professional/sites/10/Getting-Started-Guide-for-Students-English.pdf

[4] These information refer to the first variables presented when opening the websites of the Office for National Statistics (https://www.ons.gov.uk/) in the UK or the Bureau of Labor Statistics in the US (https://www.bls.gov/), respectively.

Fama (1990) seminal paper investigates the relation between equity returns and inflation. He first documented a negative relation between the two, driven by the negative relation between inflation and real activity. However, that negative relation disappears when the rate of inflation is separated into the expected and the unexpected component. Fama (1990)'s paper, and many others afterwards,[5] highlights the relevance of macroeconomic variables in influencing stock returns. A different line of that literature advanced further to examine the question of what happens on the day the market is updated on macroeconomic variables.

Boyd et al. (2005) present a detailed analysis of the reaction of stock prices to macroeconomic news. Considering the Bureau of Labor Statistics' (BLS) monthly announcements[6] of unemployment news, stock returns strongly depend on whether the economy is expanding or contracting. On average, the stock market responds positively to rising employment during expansionary cycles and negatively at times of downturns. That paper, however, doesn't reconcile with the work of, for example, Savor and Wilson (2013). Savor and Wilson (2013) make use of similar data across different macroeconomic variables and find that macroeconomic announcement days carry on average a positive premium. Savor and Wilson (2013) include: CPI, PPI, employment, and FOMC announcements from 1958 to 2009. Their analysis covered 1450 announcement days, versus 11,641 non-announcement days. Stock market excess returns (in excess of the risk-free rate) are about 11 basis points compared to 2 basis points on non-announcement days.

Savor and Wilson (2013) claim that macroeconomic announcement days are "special" days on the markets compared to non-announcement days. The logical and consequent question is why? Hu et al. (2022) proposed an explanation revolving around the uncertainty caused by these upcoming announcements and its resolution once the information is released. Their work points out unique risk-return patterns: large pre-announcement returns with small variances, followed by small post announcement returns with large variances. They found an important reduction of the VIX Index[7] in the aftermath of the announcements, which is consistent with the resolution of uncertainty. They sort announcement days based on the level of the VIX Index during the pre-announcement day window and found a considerable amount of premium for days that carried a higher level of the index, which is consistent with higher uncertainty among market participants.

[5] See among many (Boudoukh & Richardson, 1993).

[6] For more details on BLS data and resources see: https://www.bls.gov/

[7] The VIX Index, also known as the CBOE Volatility Index, is a measure of volatility computed with the implied volatility of the S&P500 index option prices. Created by the Chicago Board Options Exchange (CBOE), the VIX is often referred to as the "fear index" because it tends to spike during periods of market uncertainty. For more information see: https://www.cboe.com/tradable_products/vix/

4.3.1 The FOMC Puzzle

FOMC announcements have been deeply scrutinized by a large part of the literature on macroeconomic announcements. Many studies turn their attention to their effects rather than giving specific attention to other public disclosures such as job market unemployment news. Research attention to the FOMC announcements and the coined term "FOMC Puzzle" started with the seminal study of Lucca and Moench (2015). The paper, titled the "Pre-FOMC Announcement Drift" focuses on analysing the financial market behaviour prior to the FOMC announcement, specifically the day before until the announcement time. What they found is that a significant amount of equity risk premium was realized in the window of 1 and ½ trading day around the announcement period.

The aftermath of the announcement didn't underline any statistically significant reversal for several days afterwards. To fully understand the extent of this phenomenon there are some information that need to be recalled on the communication policy of the FED (a full discussion is presented previously in Chap. 2). Since 1994 the FED started to schedule regularly 8 FOMC announcements per year. Lucca and Moench (2015) research focuses on pre-scheduled meetings observed after 1994. Their sample excludes emergency meetings and conference calls: these were frequent during the 2008 financial crisis and in a few other extraordinary moments. Pre-scheduled meetings are expected by market participants, which is the core of the explanation of this phenomenon. From the opening of the market until the announcement time (usually happening around 2:15 pm), the market advances by an average of 50 basis points, which is equivalent to an annual average of 3.9%. It turns out that the outcome on the S&P 500 excess return is a large part of the annual overall realized return in the broad US stock market index. The dashed line shows what happens during the rest of trading days (non-FOMC days).

The result was obviously puzzling for several reasons:

- The amount realized happens prior to the announcement, therefore independent from the content of the announcement. No other macroeconomic announcement is preceded by such a run-up, as most of daily returns are observed during the trading day.
- There is no reversal in daily returns, and no heightened risk level is displayed. The volatility on the day before the announcement is typically U-shaped, thus rather singular than any other day.
- Although time series returns are regressed against a battery of potential explanatory variables, announcement day returns retain their highly significant impact.

A given potential explanation of pre-announcement drift is higher systematic risk in those days, as FED releases are interpreted as signals about future consumption growth and their impact on asset prices. Announcements might positively surprise investors since the general trend of the Federal Fund Target Rate was overall negative throughout their sample period (1994–2011). Their work initiated a stream of literature that started to take a closer look at FOMC announcements. The research agenda has been mostly directed at understanding why and how they were "special", compared to other macro announcements and general trading days.

The literature focused on different approaches to further investigate that research field: (i) broadening the sample period; (ii) looking at the type of assets affected by policy disclosure; (iii) the degree of persistence of FOMC premium across years; (iv) how wide information asymmetry is on those days; and (v) the cross-sectional effects on stock returns. The literature becomes, obviously, of particular interest to market participants, given the investment performances that could be realized around those days as well as the implications for the whole spectrum of asset pricing. Cieslak et al. (2019) document that the premium is entirely earned around the even weeks of the "FOMC Cycle". Their conclusion is obtained because they study the returns throughout the period in between meeting dates. To prove the existence of these cycles and the fact that they are driven by the FOMC announcement, they report several pieces of evidence. First, they show that Federal Fund Futures decline in even weeks, consistent with good news. Second, stock returns are particularly high on the even-week days that also have more FED information production and decision making. Specifically, they document higher even-week returns on days that follow FED board meetings.

As mentioned earlier, the economic significance is connected to the trading strategy that could be designed to take advantage of the empirical evidence. Specifically, they present and compare the performances of three different strategies. A first strategy is simply going long the stock market at all times and yields 8.48% per year, with an annual volatility of about 19% and a Sharpe ratio[8] of 0.45, which translates to an additional 0.45% return for each additional unit of risk (standard deviation) that we are undertaking. A second strategy only invests in the even weeks of the FOMC cycle. The strategy is feasible, since FOMC meetings are pre-scheduled and Exchange Traded Funds on the S&P500 provide a viable and cheaper financial instrument to make those investments (Cieslak et al., 2019). The Sharpe ratio of this strategy climbs up to 0.92. The last strategy shows that the negative returns of odd weeks could benefit the strategy if implemented with a short position.

Is the FOMC premium homogenous across time? Kurov et al. (2021) document that when extending the sample to 2019, the FOMC premium was almost disappearing after 2015. Between 2016 and 2019 the drift disappears, with cumulative premia that aren't statistically significantly different from zero. The previous strategy of Cieslak et al. (2019) only included results with a sample up to 2016. These last results show the non-persistency of Lucca and Moench (2015) work and potentially also the non-viability of the strategies proposed by Cieslak et al. (2019). That latest paper is more focused on explaining the motivation and investigating the cross-section of stock returns rather than expanding the sample of analysis. For example, recently Liu et al. (2022) examine the recovery and prediction of the premium,

[8] The Sharpe Ratio is a widely used measure of return to risk ratio in finance. The Sharpe Ratio is employed by investor to evaluate the risk-adjusted return of an investment portfolio. The measure was developed by Sharpe (1966). The measure relates the Risk Premium of a Portfolio to its standard deviation.

focusing on the pre-pandemic periods. Differently, Ai et al. (2023) analyse recent data up to 2023 to study macroeconomic announcements (as described in the previous subsection).

One interesting result of the literature on macroeconomic announcements, and specifically of the effects of FOMC announcement days, is the finding of the efficiency of the Capital Asset Pricing Model. A vast literature has been showing the inconsistency of theoretical model predictions with market data (see evidence and a thorough discussion in Fama-French, 1992). Thus, the CAPM does not yield results consistent with theory during normal trading days, but apparently displays good performances during announcement days. Savor and Wilson (2014) first document this phenomenon and find that the premium was largely correlated with the systematic risk measured through stock market betas. This is consistent with the heightened systematic risk explanation proposed by Lucca and Moench (2015). Specifically, they found that on announcement days about inflation and unemployment, the FOMC stock market beta is economically and statistically significantly related to returns on individual stocks.

Ai et al. (2022) extend further their research in the field by showing that monetary policy announcements require a significant risk compensation in the cross-section of equity returns. They propose a sensitivity measure of stocks to monetary policy announcements and find that a long-short portfolio generates an average of 31 bps of excess return per announcement day.

What is interesting about this strand of academic research is the strong applicability to investment strategy and the potential impact it can have on the financial industry. As of now, most of the discussion in this chapter has been focused on stock returns. However, a portion of the literature has focused on other metrics, such as volume and volatility, and even other asset classes (e.g., bonds and currencies).

A notable example is the study of Bollerslev et al. (2018), that employs the arrival of an FOMC announcement as a setting to understand how financial markets process the arrival of information. Their focus is on the volatility-volume relationship around the announcement day. As shown in Figure XX, the volume intensity and volatility intensity post-event are both considerably higher than pre-event.

When studying the relationship between the log volume and log volatility jumps, however, the ratio is largely below the unit, showing an inelastic relationship. Bollerslev et al. (2018)'s results are consistent with the agreement-disagreement that might develop around announcement days. The elasticity observed on days surrounding public announcements is given by the difference in opinions when news hit markets. That shows two important facts: on the one hand, how market processes information during FOMC announcement days, and on the other that elasticity is largely dependent on the difference of opinions among market participants.

Turning attention to different asset classes and financial investment types, the literature has mostly focused on bonds and currencies. Some initial evidence is also available on the observed movements in cryptocurrencies. Ahn and Melvin (2007) pioneered a study that looks at FOMC announcements and intra-day exchange rates movements, showing the "switch" between informed and uninformed trading.

Mueller et al. (2017) find first evidence of a statistically significant premium for different currencies versus the US dollar.

Announcement days display a statistically significant premium, compared to non-announcement days. Consistently with Lucca and Moench (2015), the premium is related to trading movements in the exchange rates rather than to interest rate changes. What is clear is that the difference between returns earned on announcement and non-announcement days is larger for currencies that have higher interest rate differentials vis-à-vis the United States. Consistent with the findings on returns, volatility is heightened around the announcement times.

Those results are consistent with previous studies that have been ultimately focusing on portfolio strategies that aim to exploit the premia. Therefore, considering earlier results on currencies with low or high interest rate differential vis-à-vis the US, they construct portfolios with similar characteristics. Portfolio returns track known trading strategies and obtain comparable performances as measured through Sharpe Ratios. However, when compared to carry trades, which display negative skewness, those strategies display positive skewness.

Yet, all the accumulated evidence of the effects of FOMC disclosure on financial markets has been difficult to reconcile with standard asset pricing model. Or, more simply, what are the theoretical grounds for investors to behave differently around these days? What it is clear from the evidence shown is that systematic risk might be heightened, and investors might require a higher premium to hold stocks or any other risky assets around those days. Ai and Bansal (2018) developed a revealed preference theory for the equity premium around macroeconomic announcements. Ultimately, they demonstrate that generalized risk sensitivity is exactly the class of preferences that demands a risk compensation for news that affects continuation utilities. Pflueger and Rinaldi (2022) show that endogeneous variation in risk aversion over the business cycle explains the response to high-frequency monetary policy shocks, which can be reconciled with standard asset pricing models.

Most available empirical results that I review in this chapter refer to pre-Covid-19 pandemic time, but at the time of this writing we don't have sufficient evidence of what happened during and after the 2020–2021 health crisis. We now have 4 years of FOMC announcements, S&P500 daily returns, and VIX Index daily changes. We report some summary statistics in Table 4.1. Consistent with the literature and Kurov (2021) the FOMC announcements premium is considerably reduced (mostly negative) in the post-pandemic times. The reason could be related to the negative sentiment that has been prevailing in financial markets as well as the consequent interest rates hikes (Table 4.1).

What remains validated from pre-pandemic results is that the overall FOMC announcements still carry a premium 3x higher than non-announcement days with a lower standard deviation. Similarly, the drop in the VIX, consistent with the discussed studies, is considerably higher than what is observed during non-announcement days. The pattern reported by Hu et al. (2022) is confirmed, even though it is much smaller in size and statistical significance.

4.3.2 The FOMC Puzzle and International Evidence

The primary interest of the reviewed literature so far has been on the FOMC announcements and their impact on the US economy. It is no mystery that most of the undergoing research is done on the United States and that the FED as a central bank holds a very important place in the world economy. Further, FED decisions outmatch all other major central banks. There is much less research on the announcements of the ECB and the BOE, and most of the findings point to the conclusion that their announcements do not carry the premium that characterized the FOMC announcements.

Brusa et al. (2020) are the first study that makes a comparison of central banks announcement effects by using FOMC, ECB, BOE, and Bank of Japan (BOJ) data. Their sample period covers the years 1998 to 2016, when those monetary policymakers were independent and held regular scheduled meetings. They all pursued active monetary policy while allowing their currencies to free-floating in financial markets. What we learn from that study is that FOMC announcements retain a significant premium effect on international financial markets. Surprisingly, often that higher premium is detected at FOMC announcement than when the domestic central bank speaks up. Their paper analyses more than 20 countries, using Datastream Global Country return indices.

Among others, the UK market on average jumps at FED announcements, whereas it doesn't seem to care about its own national central bank announcement. Should not the domestic financial market mostly be concerned with the domestic monetary policymakers? Ultimately, they retain the power to first influence short-term interest rate markets and the consequent risk premia. Why are the US policymakers "ruling" international financial markets? Brusa et al. (2020) proposed a few explanations. In the first, they argue there is a surprise effect. When market participants are hit by FOMC news, they typically get positively surprised. Brusa et al. (2020)'s research covers a time span that includes both the "Greenspan Put" and the subsequent "Bernanke Put" times, which refer to monetary policy cycles when the FED was stepping in to supporting markets. Past FED Chair Janet Yellen is known for a famous statement in 2013 when disclosing that the Bank would "diminish that support". That statement was intended to clarify that the FED works through financial markets but not "for" financial markets.

Brusa et al. (2020) controlled their analysis for the Bernanke and Kuttner (2005) surprise. To address surprise announcements of the ECB, BOJ, and BOE, they employed the EURIBOR, Euroyen TIBOR, and Sterling LIBOR, respectively. The FED coefficient is statistically significant across all the countries, showing a positive response to FOMC surprises. On the contrary, other central banks surprises are not positively perceived by financial markets. Ultimately, however, surprises do not explain the international reaction to FOMC announcements. Brusa et al. (2020) conclude that the FED stands for a unique importance across global investors.

4.3.3 Macroeconomic Attention

Research work that we review so far has been converging to the conclusion that FOMC announcements rank highly as some of the most anticipated and scrutinized macroeconomic events in financial markets. These events are characterized by a high level of information asymmetry among investors, and the arrival of central bank disclosure statements help to resolve that asymmetry. Similarly to what is observed in other financial market settings, that resolution comes with the reaction of investors that generates a higher than average premium (Tetlock, 2010, 2011). One implication of this accepted "stylized fact" in monetary policy literature is related to the role played by investors' attention when reacting to these important events.

In a different market surprise setting, Barber and Odean (2008) uncover that investors are buyers of "attention-grabbing" stocks. Does that evidence get also observed at times of macroeconomic announcements? There exist some recent papers that present evidence consistent with that behaviour.

For example, Boguth et al. (2019) uncover that investors pay lower attention to FOMC announcement meetings which are not followed by a press-release. In Chap. 3, I noticed that the FED communication strategy has considerably changed in the past 3 decades. That change has got academic research interest. Thus, research started to investigate whether that had an impact on financial market reactions, and specifically to clarify and perhaps better understand the effects of disclosed information. Boguth et al. (2019) focused on the 2011–2017 announcement period, with 27 announcements followed by a Press Conference and 25 meetings that were not.

Boguth et al. (2019) also focused on the attention level prior to the FOMC announcements, using active and passive forms of investor attention. They define a passive form of investor attention when media outlets are involved, whereas an active form of investor attention is when they engage with Google Search Index (SVI) (Da et al., 2011). They uncover strong evidence that all forms of investor attention shifted since the introduction of press conferences. However, investors do not spread their attention equally across the 8 pre-scheduled FOMC announcements.

Fisher et al. (2022) are an example of a study that proposes Macroeconomic Attention Indexes (MAI). MAI are new measures of attention to different macroeconomic risks, frequently proxied by a mixture of macroeconomic variables. MAI indexes are based on the number of daily articles and news that cover macroeconomic announcements, as a percentage of the total number of published articles in outlets such as the New York Times and the Wall Street Journal.

Overall in their work, it is noticeable that attention is inversely proportional to the performance of macro variables. More simply, investors seem to be worried about macroeconomic variables during downturns, whereas they are less interested in following them in good times. For example, the graph related to "Monetary Policy", shows an obvious spike in attention after the financial crisis and throughout the ZLB period. They conclude that attention provides prediction on premia as well as implied volatility changes with large economic magnitudes.

Monaco and Murgia (2023) focused on the heightened premium generated by FOMC announcements with a novel measure of attention constructed with the SVI. Their attention index spans the 5-day window around the FOMC meetings and has proven to predict and "boost" the premium associated with it. Similarly, attention is typically associated with a higher reduction in uncertainty and implied volatility estimated with the VIX index. Summing up, macroeconomic variables attention in financial markets, even though is not ***causal*** to the higher premium, is a valuable predictor as well as a potential boost around central bank announcement times.

References

Ahn, S. C., & Melvin, M. (2007). Exchange rates and FOMC days. *Journal of Money Credit and Banking, 39*(5), 1003–1283.

Ai, H., & Bansal, R. (2018). Risk preferences and the macroeconomic announcement premium. *Econometrica, 86*(4), 1383–1430.

Ai, H., Han, L. J., Pan, X. N., & Xu, L. (2022). The cross section of the monetary policy announcement premia. *Journal of Financial Economics, 143*(1), 247–276.

Ai, H., Bansal, R., & Guo, H. (2023). *Macroeconomic announcement premium*. NBER Working Paper Series, 1–36.

Barber, B. M., & Odean, T. (2008). All that glitters: The effect of attention and news on the buying behavior of individual and institutional investors. *Review of Financial Studies, 21*(2), 785–818.

Bernanke, B. S., & Kuttner, K. N. (2005). What explains the stock market's reaction to Federal Reserve Policy? *Journal of Finance, 60*(3), 1221–1257.

Boguth, O., Gregoire, V., & Martineau, C. (2019). Shaping expectations and coordinating attention: The unintended consequences of FOMC press conferences. *Journal of Financial and Quantitative Analysis, 54*(6), 2327–2353.

Bollerslev, T., Li, J., & Xue, Y. (2018). Volume, volatility and public news announcements. *Review of Economic Studies, 85*(1), 2005–2041.

Boudoukh, J., & Richardson, M. (1993). Stock returns and inflation: A long-horizon perspective. *American Economic Review, 83*(5), 1346–1355.

Boyd, J. H., Hu, J., & Jagannathan, R. (2005). The stock market's reaction to unemployment news: Why bad news is usually good for stocks. *Journal of Finance, 60*(2), 649–672.

Brusa, F., Wilson, S., & Savor, P. (2020). One Central Bank to rule them all. *Review of Finance, 24*, 263–304.

Cieslak, A., Morse, A., & Vissing-Jorgensen, A. (2019). Stock returns over the FOMC cycle. *Journal of Finance, 74*(5), 2201–2248.

Cook, T., & Hahn, T. (1989). The effect of changes in the federal funds rate target on market interest rates in the 1970s. *Journal of Monetary Economics, 24*(3), 331–351.

Da, Z., Engelberg, J., & Gao, P. (2011). In search of attention. *Journal of Finance, 66*(5), 1461–1499.

Fama, E. F. (1970). Efficient capital markets: A review of theory and empirical work. *The journal of Finance, 25*(2), 383–417.

Fama, E. F. (1990). Stock return, real activity, inflation and money. *Journal of Finance, 45*(4), 1089–1108.

Fama, E. F., & French, K. (1992). The cross-section of expected stock returns. *Journal of Finance, 47*(2), 427–465.

Fisher, A., Martineau, C., & Sheng, J. (2022). Macroeconomic attention and announcement risk Premia. *The Review of Financial Studies, 35*(11), 5057–5093.

Hu, G. X., Pan, J., Wang, J., & Zhu, H. (2022). Premium for heightened uncertainty: Explaining pre-announcement market returns. *Journal of Financial Economics, 145*(3), 909–936.

Kurov, A. (2021). The disappearing pre-FOMC announcement drift. *Finance Research Letters, 40*(1), 1–4.

Kurov, A., Wolfe, M. H., & Gilbert, T. (2021). The disappearing pre-FOMC announcement drift. *Finance research letters, 40*, 101781.

Kuttner, K. N. (2001). Monetary policy surprises and interest rates: Evidence from the Fed funds futures market. *Journal of Monetary Economics, 47*(3), 523–544.

Kyriazis, A., Ofeidis, I., Palaiokrassas, G., & Tassiulas, L. (2023). *Monetary policy, digital assets, and DeFi activity*. Cornell University Working Papers, 1–33.

Liu, H., Tang, X., & Zhou, G. (2022). Recovering the FOMC premium. *Journal of Financial Economics, 145*(1), 45–68.

Lucca, D. O., & Moench, E. (2015). The pre-FOMC announcement drift. *The Journal of Finance, 70*(1), 329–371.

Monaco, E., & Murgia, L. M. (2023). Retail attention and the FOMC equity premium. *Finance Research Letters, 53*(1), 1–6.

Mueller, P., Tahbaz-Salehi, A., & Vedolin, A. (2017). Exchange rates and monetary policy uncertainty. *Journal of Finance, 72*(3), 1213–1252.

Pflueger, C., & Rinaldi, G. (2022). Why does the Fed move markets so much? A model of monetary policy and time-varying risk aversion. *Journal of Financial Economics, 146*(1), 71–89.

Savor, P., & Wilson, M. (2013). How much do investors care about macroeconomic risk? Evidence from scheduled economic announcements. *The Journal of Financial and Quantitative Analysis, 48*(2), 343–375.

Savor, P., & Wilson, M. (2014). Asset pricing: A tale of two days. *Journal of Financial Economics, 113*(1), 171–201.

Sharpe, W. F. (1966). Mutual fund performance. *Journal of Business, 39*(1), 119–138.

Tetlock, P. C. (2010). Does public financial news resolve asymmetric information? *The Review of Financial Studies, 23*(9), 3520–3557.

Tetlock, P. C. (2011). All the news that's fit to reprint: Do investors react to stale information? *The Review of Financial Studies, 24*(5), 1481–1512.

Chapter 5
How Do We Measure the Economic Impact of Monetary Policy?

5.1 Introduction

Although the title of this chapter is a very straightforward question, the answer requires an in-depth analysis. Since the US economic recession experienced during Fed Chair Volcker it has become clear to researchers that it was imperative to understand the effects of a sudden tight monetary policy. The crises that have followed and the development of monetary policy institutions have contributed to shaping and directing the identification strategies for monetary shocks and their effects. In this chapter, I review the early vector autoregressive approaches that have become the pillar of this literature since the Sims (1980) ground-breaking paper. Next, I'll look at further literature developments and expand to the newest methodologies which are mainly focusing on the use of external instruments.

Ramey (2016) is a comprehensive review of early methodologies developed to identify shocks and their propagation. However, further extensions have been presented in the literature. Therefore, an in-depth examination is required as the recent empirical findings shed light on the propagation effects in the economy, which are particularly relevant given the current worldwide shift in monetary policy approaches. It is also appropriate to remember that the empirical research methodologies developed in the last decades have been following and adjusting to the setting of monetary policy and its available instruments, whilst adapting to exogenous events brought by the dynamics of economic and financial cycles.

However, before discussing the influence of economic and financial cycles, it could be helpful to recollect some terminology that refers to the main variables of interest discussed in this chapter.

- A *Monetary Policy Innovation (MPI)* refers to change in the current monetary policy. This term has been often used to refer to a change in the current level of the central bank reference interest rate (i.e., the Federal Funds Target rate in the

L. M. Murgia, *The Impact of Monetary Policy*, Financial and Monetary Policy Studies 56, https://doi.org/10.1007/978-3-032-15451-4_5

case of the FED, or the main refinancing rate for the ECB, or the base rate for the Bank of England).[1]

- A *Monetary Policy Shock (MPS)* refers to the unexpected component of a MPI, which is estimated as the residual of a reduced form VAR.[2] According to early literature (e.g., Ramey, 2016) shocks should have the following characteristics: (i) exogenous with respect to other model variables; (ii) shouldn't be equivalent or anticipated by other exogenous shocks, otherwise the single causality effect could be questioned; (iii) it should encompass unanticipated future movements or news.

The two terms refer mainly to the employment of conventional monetary policy tools and the ability of central bankers to influence or change the level of the reference interest rates. The subsequent literature has been debating and directing its attention to the question "Why focus on MPS and not simply on MPI?" Christiano et al. (1999) confront that question by advocating the necessity to restrain endogeneity and other confounding effects:

> …monetary policy actions reflect, in part, policy makers' responses to nonmonetary developments in the economy. A given policy action and the economic events that follow it reflect the effects of all the shocks to the economy.

Since the 2008–2009 global financial crisis, monetary policy tools and interventions have been extensively debated among academic and industry experts, particularly when judging their boundaries and efficacy. When the concept of "systemic" was first introduced in monetary policy debates, central bankers had to coordinate to present a united front and re-establish financial stability. Davies (2014) inquires into the origins and consequences of financial crises and suggests that the support to global financial stability was inadequate during the summer of 2007. However, the existing network of regulators ultimately agreed to the principle of achieving consensus. More recently, Bernanke (2022), when reviewing his assessment of the great financial crisis lessons, singles out that both the shadow-banking system cascade effects and public panic were the novel facts. However, he also clarifies that, "they were rather an old story with new clothes".

Global monetary policy responses to the financial crisis introduced a series of new action plans. The FED advanced in researching new tools and instruments, being rather creative in designing new policies. The ECB was heavily criticized for its "slow" response to the financial crisis, even though its circumstances were affected by a complicated setting on the fiscal and liquidity fronts of a rather heterogeneous and continually squabbling group of countries. The joint and officially coordinated responses by the FED, the BOE, and the ECB relied initially on conventional monetary policy tools and sharp cuts in their reference interest rates. Analysing the impact of changes in reference interest rate levels has proven

[1] Bernanke and Mihov (1998) first employed this term when advocating the use of Vector Autoregressive methodologies to measure monetary policy and its effect on the macroeconomy.

[2] Christiano et al. (1996) used this terminology when developing their series of monetary shocks in an attempt to control for endogeneity and anticipatory effects.

challenging for researchers. However, even more complicated was analysing the effects of unconventional monetary policy tools that came next.

The zero-lower bound (ZLB) period has also presented new challenges for econometricians as MPI were no longer an available variable for almost a decade. A complication of the after-crisis period was the Eurozone situation presented by the solvency issue posed by Greece, which ultimately led to the European Sovereign Debt Crisis of 2011–2012. The subsequent period of 2016–2019 was characterized by the uncertainty about how to conduct monetary policy and the growing concern over the increasing size of central bank balance sheets. The Covid-19 pandemic, which exploded in 2020–2021, is not yet well incorporated into the literature on monetary shocks. Although the pandemic crisis is considered one of the biggest global shocks observed in modern times, a limited number of published articles that have looked at its consequences are currently available.

There are two aspects to be noticed. The first is that the cut in the interest rate levels worldwide was less pronounced compared to those prior to the Global Financial Crisis.

Figure 5.1 presents the path of interest rates from January 1997 until July 2023 for the United Kingdom (the Bank Rate) and for the United States (the Federal Funds Target rate). The figure clearly displays the fall of interest rates across 2007–2008 (the timing is slightly different for the Federal Reserve and the Bank of England, since the Bank of England cut interest rates as a reaction to the meltdown in the United States). The drop was about −5% in both economies, leading to the

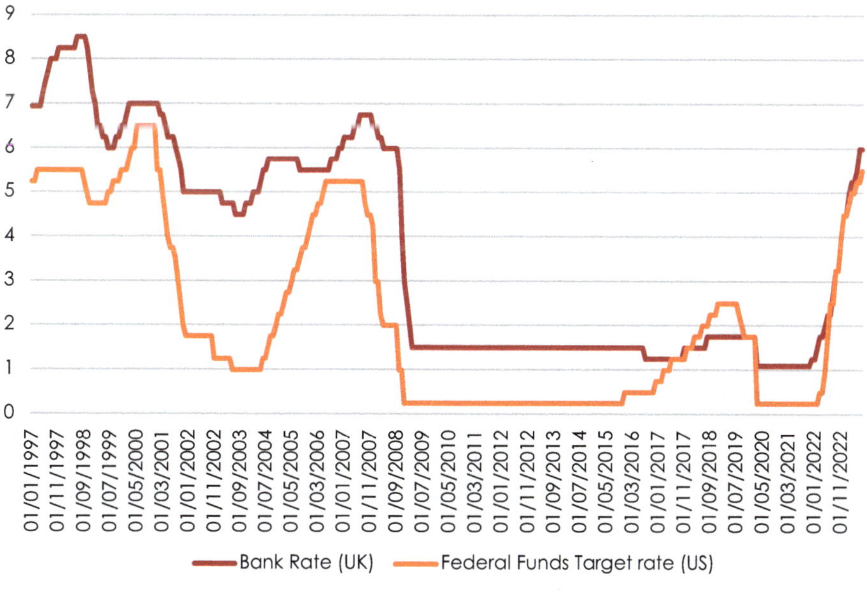

Fig. 5.1 Interest rate path. The figure plots the reference interest for the United Kingdom (Bank Rate - UK) and for the United States (Federal Funds Target rate—US) from January 1997 until July 2023. Source: FRED and Bank of England

ZLB. Until 2019 both central banks managed to start the "careful recovery" of interest rates that peaked at 2.5% in the United States and 1.75% in the United Kingdom. The pandemic practically restored the ZLB in the United States, even though the starting point is considerably lower than at the time of the explosion of the Financial Crisis, as well as in the international economic environment.

The second aspect that should be highlighted is that the Global Financial Crisis originated in financial markets, which are typically considered a leading economic indicator. Subsequently the crisis cascaded to the real economy and therefore lagging indicators, such as the unemployment rate. What was an unexpected event is that the Covid-19 pandemic crisis originated from an unexpected trajectory: it followed exactly the opposite path. Because monetary policy and macroeconomic variables are endogenously related, the analysis of the effectiveness of monetary policy at times of the Covid-19 pandemic shock would need to account for the "inverse path" of such a unique, one-time, macroeconomic shock.

As discussed in the first chapter, alongside the economic changes and challenges that have characterized the last two decades, policymakers have also changed their public disclosure policies. This aspect stands for a further challenge in the estimation of unanticipated MPS, due to the confounding effects and anticipatory movements resulting from innovations in the disclosure policy.

5.2 Assessing the Impact of Monetary Policy Shocks: Early Vector Autoregressive Approaches

The revolutionary work of Sims (1980) made the link between innovations to a linear system and macroeconomic shocks (Ramey, 2016). His work was the first to introduce the VAR approach. That approach is presented in the following Eq. (5.1):

$$Y_t = B(L)Y_{t-1} + \varepsilon_t,\ t = 1,\ldots,T, \tag{5.1}$$

where $B(L)$ is a polynomial with a set number of Lags and ε_t are the one step ahead prediction errors with a variance-covariance matrix $\sum$. Usually, a constant and a time trend are added to the analysis. The specific literature will be examined in this section. The VAR literature approach has explored various modification, particularly regarding the decomposition of ε_t to estimate the simultaneous effect of macroeconomic variables within a sample period.

Further, Sims (1992) led the way in employing vector autoregressive (VAR) methodologies, and advocated their use compared to existing macroeconomic analyses. Additionally, he employed a multi-country dataset, including France, Germany, Japan, the United Kingdom, and the United States. Sims (1992) first VAR model included a short-term interest rate, a monetary aggregate, a consumer price index, an industrial production index, an exchange rate measure, and a commodity price index. It is important to remark that Sims's baseline VAR model is still adopted in more recent studies.

It is also important to point out that the Sims (1992) study started a different path when identifying monetary policy instruments. Sims's paper was the first to bring attention to the role of short-term interest rates as a monetary policy instrument. Existing literature at that time was mostly based on changes in the stock of money. Later empirical research, such as Bernanke and Mihov (1998), further demonstrated the importance of choosing the right monetary policy instrument. Bernanke and Mihov (1998) show that money stock is unsuitable for efficient and accurate testing of those empirical models. A VAR model outcome is the impulse response function (IRF), which is a key empirical finding when searching for the correct identification of the transmission of monetary policy to the economy.

Sims (1992)'s most important result is now a stylized fact in this area of research: a contractionary monetary policy innovation is followed by a sharp decline in economic output and money stock. Sims (1992)'s results were easy to reconcile with the IS-LM monetarist theory. His results that did not fit the theory's predictions were largely a consequence of the consumer price index response. The IRFs of consumer prices display a counterintuitive first increase when a contractionary monetary policy decision is adopted. Sims (1992) addresses these results, which were alike across his international sample. His most important contribution has been to direct attention to important model design that will affect future empirical studies. First, he asserts the need to include commodity prices and exchange rates to correctly identify the affected price system. Second, the results will be later known as the "Price Puzzle" (Eichenbaum, 1992). Since then a large amount of research efforts have been undertaken to advance the Sims VAR model approach, with all studies united in achieving a solution to the price puzzle.

The subsequent empirical research has been mainly focused on the proper identification of the correct monetary policy instruments and the combination of variables to be included in the VAR and its model design. Christiano et al. (1996), for example, focused on the United States economy and employed a similar identification strategy with two separate measures of monetary policy shocks. The main goal of their work was to find the causality of exogenous shocks and at the same time to avoid the endogeneity issue first identified by Sims (1992). To achieve those objectives, they employ orthogonalized shocks to the Federal Funds rate and to nonborrowed reserves. The orthogonality property of monetary shocks has become a standard methodological approach in the empirical analyses. Researchers have been placing significant efforts into proving the orthogonality of their shock series.

That monetary shock property sets up the assumption that the researcher can isolate the effect of the central bank policy actions (such as the FED in Christiano et al., 1996), which are deemed to be exogenous to macroeconomic variables. A monetary policy shock is, in other words, the disturbance term in the monetary policy function of the policymakers. Christiano et al. (1996) formalized that idea in the following equation:

$$S_t = \Psi(\Omega_t) + \sigma\varepsilon_{st} \tag{5.2}$$

The policy instrument S_t is a linear function of the Ω_t information set available to the monetary authority. What is important to notice is that the information set $\Psi(\Omega_t)$ is assumed to be available at the same time when setting of S_t. For example, a time at which S_t is set is one of the 8 pre-scheduled FOMC meetings when the Federal Funds Target rate is decided. The orthogonality condition is built upon the assumption that the monetary policy decision does not affect policymakers information set. That assumption makes it possible to address the endogeneity concerns.

Christiano et al. (1999), following Sims (1992)'s "recursive VAR approach", after a monetary policy shock, document a severe and persistent decline in real GDP, employment, and corporate profits in nonfinancial sectors. Furthermore, they reaffirm the importance of including commodity prices when modelling to resolve the "Price Puzzle".

The study of Christiano et al. (1999) contributed to a complete review of the methodological literature that had been dealing with the question "What happens after an exogenous shock to monetary policy?". They point to three steps to implement an effective empirical investigation:[3]:

1. Isolate monetary policy shocks from the real economy.
2. Characterize the economy's response to the shocks.
3. Perform the analysis in model economies to be evaluated and compare the outcome with actual economies.

These points must be kept in mind as they summarize the direction that research has taken in the two decades after their contribution. They name three specific strategies. The first and main point of their work is to estimate *MPS* under a "*recursive assumption*". Their claim is that shocks are orthogonal to the information set of policymakers and define the set as the actual prices and output levels. The second approach studies data and names specific events to be "candidates" for monetary shocks, as in Romer and Romer (1989). The third and last research effort is to estimate monetary shocks under the assumption that they will not affect the economy in the long run.

Their review also emphasizes some stylized facts in the literature: "after a contractionary monetary policy shock, short-term interest rates rise, aggregate output, employment, profits, and various monetary aggregates fall, the aggregate price level responds very slowly, and various measures of wages fall, albeit by very modest amounts".

Once again it is worth bringing back to the discussion that it is more important to focus on MPS than on MPI. However, despite the literature accepted view, it is intellectually honest to remark that MPS only accounts for very little volatility in both output and prices, showing that the models' explanatory power was not yet satisfying.

[3] This also refers to the Lucas's (1980) program.

The "Recursiveness Assumption" was at the centre of the discussion of Christiano et al. (1999) and will be further carried on in the literature even when external instruments are employed in the analysis. Their model employed, in fact, a modified version of the Cholesky decomposition that included a restriction to the first lag of the macroeconomic variables that would not respond to monetary policy, but they would allow it to affect monetary policy.[4]

Recent developments in the empirical literature are on the identification and transmission of monetary shocks that require the use of external instruments. These methodologies are further discussed in the following sections. However, it could be useful to recollect that their development was strongly influenced by the mentioned model assumptions and theories as well as the development of policymakers' operating system and communication.

5.3 The Narrative Approach

The term "Narrative Identification" refers to the construction of series of monetary shocks, by using the historical narrative record from a policymaker meeting. The methodology and the terminology were first coined by Romer and Romer (1989, 2004, R&R henceforth). They constructed a series of intended changes in interest rates around the FOMC meetings. Romer and Romer (R&R) have further refined their empirical approach in very recent times (see Romer & Romer, 2023). In their first paper, the research motivation and purpose was to understand whether "nominal disturbances have important real effects", which simply is an elegant way of stating that monetary policy matters.

R&R narrative identification is based on historical meeting records, and it is distinguished from the vast statistical approach literature. Furthermore, it tackles the research question of monetary policy effects from a different perspective, and in doing so it stands up to Friedman and Schwartz's (1963) classical view of the "monetary shock". Romer and Romer (1989)'s study re-defines "monetary shocks" as "episodes in which the Federal Reserve attempted to exert a contractionary influence on the economy in order to reduce inflation". Their focus was entirely on what was considered "excessive inflation", consistent with the Inflation Targeting framework that was later embraced by major central banks (e.g.: Bank of England joined that policy framework in 1992). In a subsequent research contribution (Romer & Romer, 2004) they build up a full methodology to retrieve a monetary shock series in the United States, entirely based on the Federal Reserve proprietary forecasts that are periodically released through the "Greenbooks".[5]

[4] Ramey (2016) dedicated in his review a large discussion on the importance of the recursiveness assumption

[5] The "Greenbooks" includes the staff analysis of the U.S. and the international economy. This document was distributed about six days before the FOMC meeting. The Greenbooks were published between 1964–2010 and have now been replaced by the "Tealbooks". For more details on

This method was motivated by its ability to avoid anticipatory effects and endogeneity, by including the set of information that policymakers were taking into account when considering monetary policy decisions. To build the shock series, in fact, Romer and Romer (2004) developed the following model:

$$\Delta ff_m = \alpha + \beta\, ffb_m + \sum_{i=-1}^{2} \gamma_i\, \Delta\tilde{y}_{mi} + \sum_{i=-1}^{2} \delta_i\, (\Delta\tilde{y}_{mi} - \Delta\tilde{y}_{m-1,i}) + \sum_{i=-1}^{2} \varphi_i\, \tilde{\pi}_{mi} + \sum_{i=-1}^{2} \theta_i\, (\tilde{\pi}_{mi} - \tilde{\pi}_{m-1,i}) + \rho\, \tilde{u}_{m0} + \varepsilon_m \tag{5.3}$$

where Δff_m is the intended change in interest rates around FOMC meetings (m) as in Bernanke and Blinder (1992), Sims (1992) and Christiano et al. (1996). ffb_m is the level of interest rates prior to the meeting (m), which intends to proxy for the FOMC tendency to follow a mean-reverting path when making monetary policy changes. Δy , π , and u refer to the forecasts for inflation, real output growth, and the unemployment rate. They also include a few more control variables related to the forecast revision from the prior meeting and no more than 2 quarters ahead of forecasts. The residuals of this equation create the time series of their shocks of monetary policy between 1969 and 1996.

Taking a closer look at this equation there are two important aspects to be noticed that are not explicitly discussed in their paper. However, they are relevant to gain a better understanding of the methodology, and to the possibility of applying R&R methods by researchers in other countries and time periods. They essentially "purge" the series of changes in the interest rate (a terminology often used by academics who have further extended their work) from the information set of the FOMC at the time of their meetings, therefore separating the expected from the unexpected component of an interest rate change. The expected component is, in fact, what is settled on based on the expected economic outlook.

What is taken for granted is whether monetary policymakers are, in fact, basing their judgements on forecasts rather than current or ex-post information. The motivation to use that data is given by their method approach. A conceptual connection can be found in the work of Svensson (2003), who argues that forecast targeting is the only way for policymakers to factor in asset price developments.

Most of the comments and referencing of the Romer and Romer (2004) study point to the results they obtained when testing the effects of the newly created shock series on measures of output and prices.[6] Their findings were, in fact, that the FOMC behaved countercyclically, showing that an increase of 1% from one FOMC meeting to another of real growth would lead on average to a 29 basis point increase in the Federal Funds target rate.

There are two elements that need to be reconsidered at this point. First, Romer and Romer (2004) identified the meetings that should have been included in the sample from 1969–1996. Before 1994 the FOMC did not have pre-scheduled

historical data and transcripts of the Federal Reserve see https://www.federalreserve.gov/monetarypolicy/fomc_historical.htm

[6] The findings are reported in Table 1, page 1063 of Romer and Romer (2004).

meetings and their announcements would come without official notice or expectation. Second, the magnitude of change in the Federal Funds Target rate was entirely up to the FOMC, whereas in recent times, the "average" official change in the Federal Funds rate has been set around 25 basis points. What also emerged from their first analysis is that the FOMC resisted forecast inflation and was keener on current unemployment and forecasted output.

The fact that unemployment was the focus of the FOMC doesn't come as a surprise, since it is an explicit component of the FED mandate, as is the advancing of economic growth. What is surprising is the lack of significance in inflation. Most importantly, in trying to assess "the determinants of changes in the Federal Funds Target rate", they were only able to explain about 30% of it (see the $R^2 = 0.28$ of their analysis reported in Table 1 of Romer and Romer, 2004). The authors do not discuss the remaining 70% of the reasons for the changes in the Federal Funds Target rate. However, further applications of their methodologies in other countries will "expand" the set of information of policymakers and achieve higher explanatory power.

Their seminal work introduced a new methodology and a fresh input in this area of research. At the same time, it also shed new light on the effects of monetary shocks on both output and prices. In a second step analysis, they accounted for the implications of this monetary shock series and found a cumulative −4.3% decline in output and − 3.6% decline in prices. What was striking about these results were the magnitude and the resolution of the "price puzzle". The magnitude of their results is therefore significantly different from the literature outcomes that were known at that time.

Coibion (2012) focused on comparing early VAR approaches with findings and methods proposed in R&R (2004). However, Coibion's (2012) study could be positioned in the literature as a middle ground between past results and those presented in R&R (2004). In Figure 2 of Coibion (2012), the author reports the IRF reproduced to compare the aforementioned methodologies.

The first column "Standard VAR" reports the results of comparable VAR approaches (as discussed above), such as the work of Christiano et al. (1999). The second column is a hybrid methodology, including the R&R (2004) shocks in a recursive VAR approach, which is the middle ground found by Coibion (2012) and analysed with additional methodologies.

Ultimately his work highlights three important key elements that account for the different results. First, Romer and Romer (2004) shock estimates are much larger than those obtained through recursive VAR approaches. Second, during the years from 1979 to 1982 the Federal Reserve abandoned targeting the Federal Funds Rate. That time is important into explaining differences obtained by distinct empirical studies. Last, R&R (2004) research is sensitive to the lag specification. Coibion (2012) extracted a measure of monetary policy shocks from an estimated Taylor Rule, with time-varying parameters, which yielded results in the middle between R&R (2004) and the earlier statistical methodologies.

5.3.1 Applications of the Narrative Identification Strategy

The narrative identification strategy is executed by computing MPS in the first stage of empirical analysis and by assuming the hypothesis that policymakers have available the key information set at the time of their decision. How is that implemented by the econometrician? R&R (2004) approximate policymakers' information through US economic forecasts that are reported in the "Greenbook". The Greenbook extends to international data that permit researchers to construct cross-country estimates and other economic and monetary union estimates.

Cloyne and Hürtgen (2016) recognized the similarity between the Greenbook published by the FED and the "Inflation Report" published by the Bank of England at a quarterly frequency.[7] They borrow the R&R (2004) methods to analyse United Kingdom data and extend the VAR methodologies to more macroeconomic variables. Cloyne and Hürtgen (2016) made two important extensions to the R&R (2004) first stage VAR (see their Eq. 5.3). Their approach has been subsequently adopted in the empirical literature. First, they included the quarterly revisions to the GDP and inflation forecasts, to allow for changes in expectations. Second, they controlled for the 3 months current unemployment rate to include the current economic situation.

Their work has provided a significant contribution to the debate on the "Price Puzzle" for the United Kingdom (Dedola & Lippi, 2005; Mountford, 2005). Furthermore, they provide a comparison of the effectiveness of the narrative methodologies when applied to a smaller open economy. Their results on output, approximated by industrial production, are consistent with both the VAR literature and the empirical evidence available for the US market. The main impulse responses are computed with a parsimonious VAR, controlling for commodity prices while ordering the MPS as the last series.

Cloyne and Hürtgen (2016) also introduced inflation targeting as another important variable in their empirical design. That variable has been a key metric in the evolution of central banks' monetary policy decision process. Past studies did not include or control for inflation targeting, perhaps because of the lack of data in older sample periods. The Bank of England introduced inflation targeting in 1992, which falls into the Cloyne and Hürtgen (2016) sample. They re-estimate the MPS series by splitting the period before and after the inflation targeting framework. As predicted, the volatility of the time series shocks is largely reduced after 1992, even though the results on the macroeconomic variables remain qualitatively similar.

Champagne and Sekkel (2018) make progress in the literature on inflation targeting using Canadian data and relying on the approaches of R&R (2004) and Cloyne and Hürtgen (2016). Their study focuses, in fact, on the changes in monetary regimes and the need to account for breaks in the conduct of monetary policy when

[7] The quarterly Inflation Reports set out the economic analysis and inflation projections that the Monetary Policy Committee (MPC) uses to make its interest rate decision (more information can be found at https://www.bankofengland.co.uk/inflation-report/inflation-reports)

assessing its effect on the economy. The Bank of Canada joined the inflation targeting framework in February 1991,[8] which falls within their sample period (1974–2015).

Additionally, they extend the first stage of the methodology by including two variables measured two weeks before the Bank of Canada meeting: the Federal Funds rate level and the nominal exchange rate between the US and the Canadian dollar. That inclusion is motivated by the fact that the Canadian economy is a small open economy closely linked to the US. The interconnection between the two economies can make US monetary policy a significant driver of Canadian monetary policy. Lastly, they break the series into two subsamples to further investigate the impact of inflation targeting.

The results of the first stage regression point out significant heterogeneity in the variables' response in the two sub-periods. The overall sample analysis and the subsample prior to the inflation targeting introduction show a procyclical behaviour (with respect to output and prices) in the setting of monetary policy. Differently, in the second sub-period a countercyclical behaviour is detected. The response to the US monetary policy and exchange rates is also prominent in the pre-inflation targeting period and strongly reduced afterwards.

Further, they estimate the effects on output and prices and confirm across several tests the importance of taking into account "breaks" in the conduct of monetary policy. In particular, the estimation of the effect on prices varies substantially when the MPS employed are with or without a break in the time series. They also find that prices respond faster in a subsample analysis relating only to the inflation targeting framework, which is in line with the events that have characterized the Canadian economy between 1991 and 1994. Inflation was, in fact, close to the target very quickly after the framework was introduced.

A further application of the R&R (2004) methodology was performed in Murgia (2020) by studying the behaviour of the European Central Bank. The data on the European Central Bank proved to be methodologically more challenging given the "young age" of the institution. That data encompasses both the financial crisis and zero-lower bound periods. Removing data across those unparalleled times would not have left enough observations for the empirical analysis. Differently from studies that examine other countries where generally monetary policymakers meet 8 times per year, in the early stages of its inception, the European Central Bank Governing Council met almost every month, allowing for a richer first stage analysis. Furthermore, Murgia (2020), extended the first stage regression by including the levels of the European Central Bank total assets as a proxy for the Quantitative Easing programs.

A further application and critique of the narrative methodologies is provided by Miranda-Agrippino and Ricco (2021) by examining US data from 1991 to 2009. They combine the insights of R&R (2004) and the use of high-frequency data firstly

[8] For more detailed information on the Inflation Targeting framework see https://www.bankofcanada.ca/core-functions/monetary-policy/agreement-inflation-control-target/

proposed by Gertler and Karadi (2015).[9] That study shows that information frictions have an impact on narrative monetary surprises. However, they also uncover that those narrative surprises can be predicted with past information, and contain anticipatory effects (forward guidance). Miranda-Agrippino and Ricco (2021) ultimately proposed a new external instrument that purged the high-frequency surprises from the Greenbook forecasts, and further removed the autocorrelation component from the shock series with an AR(1) regression. It is worth mentioning that their sample period only includes the early stage of the ZLB period and encompassed the economic downturns of 2000 as well as the financial crisis in 2008.

Their results correctly identify a drop of about −1% in output, a more modest drop in prices (−0.4%), and a rise of about 0.3% in the unemployment rate. The reviewed studies conducted in different countries and during various sample periods give strong support to the narrative methodologies and their extensive use in empirical research. Most surprising is that empirical results are qualitatively similar and in line with the initial conventional wisdom across different research papers. Miranda-Agrippino and Ricco (2021) also offer an effective comparison between the use of narrative methodologies and high-frequency identification that will be further discussed in the last subsection of this chapter.

5.4 Sign-Restrictions

Whether a specification or an identification strategy yields correct results is often judged by observing whether the impulse response functions that are produced are "theoretically correct" (Ramey, 2016). For example, identifications that yield the "Price Puzzle" are per se incorrect, given that theoretically an interest rate hike should be followed by a drop in prices. To this end, several researchers have developed methodologies by investigating the effect of a shock on a certain variable X (e.g., output), where the shock was identified by imposing sign-restrictions on a set of other variables, excluding X.

The most notable study on sign-restrictions is the work developed by Uhlig (2005). Uhlig (2005) proposed a new agnostic procedure to identify the response of output (approximated with real GDP) by imposing sign-restrictions on the impulse responses of prices (to avoid the price puzzle), nonborrowed reserves, and the response of the Federal Funds rate to a monetary policy shock. The response that is not explained by the constrained model is considered "free", which means that it is the main object of the analysis and related to output.

Uhlig (2005)' s work is motivated by the "conventional wisdom" that monetary contractions should lead to:

(1) a rise in the federal funds rate
(2) lower prices

[9] The details regarding the use of high-frequency data will be discussed in the dedicated Sect. 5.5.

(3) a decrease in real output

Uhlig (2005) states that it is worthwhile to make explicit the theoretical set-up "a priori", whereas the research question should remain open, although in his paper he investigates the output reaction. His approach's main assumption is that a contractionary monetary policy shock should therefore not lead to an increase in prices, which was a point of controversy in the prior literature.

Fry and Pagan (2011) offer a critical review of the sign-restrictions methodology in monetary policy studies, which has been later adopted in other fields of research such as fiscal policy and technology shocks. In their re-examination Fry and Pagan (2011) point to the studies of Uhlig (2005), Mountford (2005), Rafiq and Mallick (2008), and Scholl and Uhlig (2008) as the more relevant advancements in this line of research. Mountford (2005) utilizes Uhlig (2005) methods with United Kingdom data and uncovers that after a contractionary monetary policy shock a persistent drop in subsequent levels of quarterly GDP is observed. Rafiq and Mallick (2008) present new results on the EMU 3 countries monetary block (Germany, France, and Italy) and investigate the hetereogeneous response of monetary policy across countries. Scholl and Uhlig (2008) apply Uhlig's approach to support the Dornbusch (1976) hypothesis and test the effects of monetary policy on exchange rates. It should be pointed out that in the recent work of Jarociński and Karadi (2020), they apply a weaker form of "sign-restriction" to identify their shocks compared to Uhlig (2005)'s method. Their restrictions are contemporaneous to the response of two variables: interest rates and the stock market dynamics. Their research combines sign-restriction and high-frequency data, so it's more appropriate to be further discussed in the next specialized subsection.

5.5 A Review of the Advent of High-Frequency Data

The identification of MPS using high-frequency (HF) data[10] has been highly discussed in the literature that examines their effects on asset prices. These shocks were, however, estimated differently, mainly following the notion of "monetary policy surprises", originally introduced by Kuttner (2001). Shocks are computed as the difference between the futures prices of the reference interest rates (mainly the Federal Funds Futures) before and after an FOMC monetary policy announcement. Equation (5.4) below exposes formally the Kuttner (2001) original idea, partially discussed in the previous chapter.[11]

[10] It is worth recalling that in macroeconomic analysis high-frequency data will include any data with a daily or higher frequency. In the financial markets microstructure research field high-frequency data will most commonly refer to data with a higher than daily frequency (see for example the dataset employed by Lucca & Moench, 2015).

[11] Equation (2.4) is a simplified version of the equation reported in Kuttner (2001) and most widely used in the literature. The original Kuttner (2001), further employed by Bernanke and Kuttner (2005) contained a scaling factor for the day in which the FOMC announcement was happening.

$$\Delta i^u = f^0_{m,d} - f^0_{m,d-1} \tag{5.4}$$

That literature is often referred to as the "market-based" identification strategy, which is mostly interested in studying how MPS impact the macroeconomy.

Bagliano and Favero (1999) derive an exogenous measure of monetary policy shocks for the US and Germany from financial market data. Their goal is to test the robustness of the traditional VAR methodologies when dealing with the issue of co-movements between the German policy interest rates and the Deutsche Mark–US dollar exchange rate. Their claim is that the recursiveness assumption of Christiano et al. (1996) is insufficient in an open economy, as is Germany, because of the simultaneous co-movement effects with the exchange rate. Their work uses as a shock the 1-month Euro-Dollar futures metric. Further, they include as a non-VAR measure and monetary shock measure the orthogonalized residual of a VAR, controlling also for several endogenous macroeconomic variables. Ultimately, their results point out the necessity of more work to "test" the robustness of VAR estimation (Rudebusch, 1998).

Cochrane and Piazzesi (2002), combining a HF identification of daily interest rates as well as the Federal Fund Target rate, "surmount painlessly" the orthogonalization problem, the time-varying parameter problem, and avoid the VAR from incorrectly interpreting anticipated actions with shocks. A particularly interesting aspect of their approach is the inclusion of financial market expectations and the "case study" analysis of the FOMC announcements around 2001. In doing so they find different results from previous studies. Their evidence shows that large unexpected changes in the Central Bank targets actually affect long-term rates such as 30-yearbond yields.

Faust et al. (2004) build their discussion on the work of both Bagliano and Favero (1999) and Cochrane and Piazzesi (2002), using derivatives markets (futures contracts) to measure the response of expected future interest rates to unexpected changes in the Federal Fund Target rate. They reject the recursive identification of Christiano et al. (1999) for being inconsistent with the Federal Funds futures market and provide compelling evidence that their analysis resolves the Price Puzzle as well (Eichenbaum, 1992; Sims, 1992). They include their surprises in the Christiano et al. (1999) 6-variable benchmark VAR.

Gürkaynak et al. (2005b) also employ monetary surprises in a similar fashion to both Kuttner (2001), Faust et al. (2004), and Cochrane and Piazzesi (2002), even though the purpose of their paper was to challenge the strong assumption made in macroeconomic models on the long-run behaviour of macroeconomic variables. Their results, particularly those on long-term yields, are in sharp contrast with established empirical literature (e.g., Romer & Romer, 2000). They find, in fact, that a positive monetary policy surprise will lead to a short-term appreciation of the long-term yield, but in the long-term (approximately after 4 years) it will reverse to a decline. This result contrasts with the macroeconomic modelling expectations that long-run properties of the economy are constant and perfectly known by all agents. They argue that the most likely explanation relies on the private-sector expectations of inflation adjustment. Their method became prominent in follow-up studies, particularly after the 2008 Financial Crisis.

Hamilton (2008) continues the discussion on the role of expectations, stating that observing what the Federal Reserve "did" by looking at the changes in the Federal Funds Target rate is irrelevant. He argues that the correct approach is to look at what they "intend to do". The revision of their intentions is, in fact, fundamental in assessing the impact on an important metric such as the mortgage market rates. His methodology measures the difference in the settlement price of daily futures contract changes, arguing that those changes can be attributed to information that flows from trading by market participants motivated by changes in interest rates and economic outlook. His methodology develops a triple-equation system to study how news on a certain day affects the level, slope, and curvature of the interest rate term structure, which usually drifts into future daily prices at the next 1, 2, and 3 settlement dates. However, taking into account the new curvature of interest rates, the novel result is that anticipated interest rate hikes will have a negative effect on new home sales and are therefore priced in mortgage rates.

Federal Funds Futures had been the main focus of HF methodologies and the most acclaimed external instrument to overcome the endogeneity issue. However, Piazzesi and Swanson (2008) criticized the then developed approaches by arguing that methodologies relying on futures prices need to be "adjusted". Their empirical results show that the "Expectations Hypothesis"(EH), which was argued to be failing for the Treasury Bill Yields (Fama & Bliss, 1987; Cochrane & Piazzesi, 2005), fails also for Federal Funds Futures, as their research discovers average positive and statistically significant excess returns. Even more surprising is their finding of a dynamic, time varying, and predictable effect. Under the EH this shouldn't be the case; excess returns on interest rates should be, in fact, constant and unpredictable by macrovariables. Piazzesi and Swanson (2008) show that these excess returns are countercyclical (when tested against a recession dummy variable, the coefficient is positive and statistically significant), and about 3 to 5 times higher than in expansion periods. The countercyclicality of risk premia arising from monetary policy announcements, which has been first documented in that paper, will be highly debated when discussing the asset pricing implications.

Before entering into the recent developments in the use of HF data to build external instruments for monetary shock series, it would be useful to recall a few key insights. First, past research employs mostly daily data, which are already considered HF in economic analysis, even though this wouldn't be the case in contemporary dynamic asset pricing research. This point is particularly relevant when we'll review those methodologies in the current and next chapters. Second, the discussed papers were developed prior to the year 2008, when the Great Financial Crisis exploded and the ZLB time started to be a significant methodological challenge for this line of research. Third, not all the reviewed studies connected the use of HF data and VAR (or Structural VAR) methodologies.

The link between VARs and HF data has been first introduced in Gertler and Karadi (2015), who looked at exogenous monetary policy surprises and quantified the joint response of a battery of economic and financial variables. The exogenous monetary policy surprises are constructed by combining the established VAR analysis (Bernanke & Blinder, 1992; Christiano et al., 1996) with HF identification (Kuttner, 2001; Gürkaynak et al., 2005a, 2005b; Hamilton, 2008). The work of Gertler and Karadi (2015) is a study that performs a different research trajectory with respect to early papers. First, they advance the use of the external instrument approach, even though their methodology based on monetary surprises mainly follows the work of Gürkaynak et al. (2005a, 2005b).

It is also worth mentioning that the extant research reviewed so far concentrates its attention on the US economy and US monetary policy, perhaps because of available tried and tested data. HF identification has grown considerably in more recent years by employing changes in interest rates and interest rate derivative futures contracts observed closely in the minutes when monetary policy announcements are made. Subsequently, new papers leverage these developed econometric methods by back-testing them on different economies. For example, Altavilla et al. (2019) provided the first comprehensive overview of the European economy and the effects of the European Central Bank policy.

Altavilla et al. (2019) employed a tick-by-tick quotes dataset to correctly disentangle the single events happening within one monetary policy announcement of the European Central Bank. Differently from the FOMC, in fact, the European Central Bank discloses the policy decision in a first moment, without a rationale for it, and only after the explanation is provided by the President of the Governing Council.[12] They also document the presence of information shocks, which had already been introduced by the work of Campbell et al. (2012) and defined as "Delphic" policy, which refers to the ability of the Federal Reserve to influence the economy without actual policy changes.

The literature debate on "information shocks" and forward guidance has later attracted the attention of other scholars such as Jarociński and Karadi (2020) and Miranda-Agrippino and Ricco (2021). As mentioned earlier, the ZLB period has been a significant challenge for researchers, since shocks based on changes in the target interest rates were no longer available in the US after 2008. Jarociński and Karadi (2020) when dissecting the monetary policy surprises found thought-inspiring results related to the ZLB period and to the reaction observed in financial markets.

What is particularly interesting in their empirical design is how they implement the link between economics and asset pricing theories. That is not entirely new, as it was used by Boyd et al. (2005), who aknowledge a "contradictory" behaviour of the stock market with regard to unemployment news. To put it simply, rising unemployment is a good news for stocks during economic expansion and bad news during

[12] See in Chap. 2 full description and discussion of the different disclosure policies of the European Central Bank and how they have developed across the years.

economic contractions. In other words, predictions of economic theory might not hold in every state of the world.

Jarociński and Karadi (2020) use the example of the FOMC rate cut on March 20, 2001. On that day the Federal Funds Target was lowered by a sizeable 50 basis point, with standard and usually expected drop in rates are only 25 basis points. The financial market should have reacted with a pronounced appreciation, as theory would predict, instead, less than an hour after the announcement shows a decline, further culminated in a loss of almost 2.5% the day after.[13] They attributed this market performance to the pessimistic information that were disclosed just afterwards with regard to the "current risks" that needed further consideration. Their work developed a HF methodology of co-movements between interest rates and the stock market in a narrow window around the moments of monetary policy announcements.

To isolate the shocks they impose sign-restrictions, stating that a negative co-movement shock is associated with an interest rate increase and a drop in stocks, whereas a positive shock is a complementary shock (positive increase in both interest rates and stock prices). They define a "Pure Monetary Policy Shock" (a negative co-movement) when the interest rates movement and the stock market co-movement are in line with theory (e.g., an interest rate cut is followed by a stock market appreciation), and a "CB Information Shock" (positive co-movement) when the interest rate movement and the stock market co-movement are dis-aligned with theoretical predictions. Ultimately, they found that the concurrent presence of these information shocks attenuates the estimated effects of monetary policy in the standard HF identification.

The study of Miranda-Agrippino and Ricco (2021), as discussed earlier, adopts the narrative methodologies, but they also enter into the discussion on information shocks and central banks' forward guidance. With respect to their HF methodology, they use data comparable to that in Altavilla et al. (2019) and Jarociński and Karadi (2020), but they also purge them as in Narrative identification strategies.

Two recent articles reconsider HF methodologies as well as the information set used to purge them, as in Miranda-Agrippino and Ricco (2021). The first is the study by Bauer and Swanson (2022) that revises the HF identification through two separate steps. Initially, they expand the set of monetary policy announcements by including speeches of the Federal Reserve Chair. Next, they explain the predictability of monetary policy surprises (previously discussed by both) using the channel further developed in Bauer and Swanson (2023). Their work revisits past methodologies in the following ways:

1. Even when HF data is used, the surprises are predictable and there is a degree of autocorrelation, that can also be overcome by orthogonalizing the time series with financial and macroeconomic variables (Miranda-Agrippino & Ricco, 2021; Bauer & Swanson, 2023).
2. Greenbook forecasts, widely used in studies adopting narrative methodologies, are not necessarily better estimators than publicly available Blue Chip Forecasts.

[13] These data refer to S&P500 performances.

> These observations challenge the view that the Federal Reserve has private information and reinforce the theory that the Federal Reserve responds to news (Bauer & Swanson, An Alternative Explanation for the "Fed Information Effect", 2023).

HF data and methodologies have, therefore, earned a prominent role as an important methodological improvement in our understanding of the effects of monetary shocks on the economy. Yet, traditional methodologies still need to be applied to reconcile results with economic theory, given the wide availability of information to the public that contributes to the predictability of the time series.

5.6 Estimation via Local Projections

The literature review conducted so far did not discuss the important issue of how the impulse responses (usually of output and prices) are treated in empirical research. The extant literature (e.g., Ramey, 2016) conducts estimation of impulse response functions of endogenous variables of interests through estimates of nonlinear function at multiple horizons from the VAR parameters. A VAR methodology can be defined as an "iterated forecasting method" (Marcellino et al., 2006; Ramey, 2016). In simple words that means iterating on a one-period ahead the estimated model. For this method to be effective the VAR cannot be mis-specified and must adequately capture the data generating process, otherwise the errors will be computed at every forecast horizon. Jordà (2005) addresses this matter by developing a "direct forecasting method" to estimate impulse responses through a single equation approach. Compared to the iterated process, a single equation approach will estimate a horizon-specific regression and parameter, which allow the misspecification of the model to be replicated over future periods. Although alternative methodologies were developed and proved to be asymptotically in line with Jordà (2005), his "Local Projections" (LPs hereafter)[14] probably are the most widely used estimation methods in macroeconomic analysis.

According to Jordà (2005) the main advantages of LPs are:

(1) they can be estimated by a simple regression model;
(2) they are robust to misspecification;
(3) the joint analytic inference is simple;
(4) they are flexible and can easily accommodate experimentation with highly non-linear variables.

How are the impulse responses estimated with LPs and compare to the impulse responses estimated with VAR methods? To address that question, it is helpful to view the LPs regression:

[14] For example, Chang and Sakata (2007) develop long autoregression methods.

$$x_{(t+h)} - x_t = c + \Psi_h(L) z_{(t-1)} + \beta_h\, shock_t + \varepsilon_{(t+h)} \text{ for } h = 0,1,2\ldots, \tag{5.5}$$

where x is the variable of interest, $z_{(t-1)}$ is a vector of lagged control variables, $\Psi_h(L)$ is a polynomial lag operator, and $shock_t$ refers to the measure of shocks and $\varepsilon_{(t+h)}$ are regression residuals. The variables of interest are the endogenous macroeconomic variables (e.g., prices and output) and control variables are those commonly adopted in the empirical literature, such as the commodity prices index, exchange rates, and credit conditions.

Jordà (2005) uses monthly data in the four decade period 1960–2001 to present a direct comparison of a set of commonly employed macrovariables. To make that contrast effective, the first important aspect is the decision on the number of lags to be implemented in the estimation procedure.[15] The first analysis is performed with a VAR of order 2, followed by a VAR of order 12. A similar number of lags was employed for the LPs. When comparing the "low-lag" analysis, Jordà (2005) observes that LPs were much more "detailed" and accurate in capturing the patterns, compared to the smoother VAR.[16]

Where were LPs applied? If I do restrain my analysis to the literature I reviewed so far, it is worth noticing that almost all the narrative methodology applications provided impulse responses estimated using LPs (among many: Cloyne & Hürtgen, 2016; Champagne & Sekkel, 2018; Miranda-Agrippino & Ricco, 2021; Romer & Romer, 2023), as well as most of the HF data studies (see, for example, the recent work of Bauer & Swanson, 2022). LPs were also re-named LP-IV when the monetary shock is unobserved, but an external instrument is employed (like a high-frequency monetary policy surprise).

A frequently obtained result in that literature is that impulse response functions estimated via LPs usually yield results of a higher size and look more "erratic". Plagborg-Møller and Wolf (2021) depart from the literature's prevailing view by cricitizing LPs and claiming that they produce the same impulse response functions as VARs. Their conclusions are supported by three main findings:

(1) LP impulse responses can be obtained by an appropriately ordered recursive VAR.
(2) Any VAR impulse response can be obtained through LPs with appropriate control variables.
(3) Treated VAR (∞) forecasts coincide with direct LP forecasts

The "requirements" for these results are that the data are weakly stationary and that the lag selection is unrestricted. Summing up, the methods can be both used for the

[15] It is common in the literature to follow the Akaike's (AIC) and Schwarz's (SC or BIC) criterions. More details on practical estimations details will be given in the next Chap. 5.

[16] What is relevant to highlight is that the error term of impulse response function estimated through LPs is the moving average of the forecast errors, thus will be serially correlated. The standard errors need to be therefore corrected for serial correlation, using methods such as Newey-West (1987).

same purpose. However, it is useful to mention that LPs estimations require to have a measure of shocks to be implemented, differently from a recursive VAR approach. The measure of shock could be estimated with a previously perfomed structural VAR (SVAR), which makes the two methods complementary. It is, in fact, worth highlighting that early papers that implemented LPs (e.g., see Miranda-Agrippino & Ricco, 2021) make use of an external instrument approach.

References

Altavilla, C., Brugnolini, L., Gürkaynak, R. S., Motto, R., & Ragusa, G. (2019). Measuring Euro area monetary policy. *Journal of Monetary Economics, 108*(1), 162–179.

Bagliano, F. C., & Favero, C. A. (1999). Information from financial markets and VAR measures of monetary policy. *European Economic Review, 43*(1), 825–837.

Bauer, M. D., & Swanson, E. T. (2022). *A reassessment of monetary policy surprises and high-frequency identification*. NBER Working Papers, 1–65.

Bauer, M. D., & Swanson, E. T. (2023). An alternative explanation for the "fed information effect". *American Economic Review, 113*(3), 664–700.

Bernanke, B. S. (2022). *21st century monetary policy: The Federal Reserve from the great inflation to COVID-19*. W.W. Norton & Company.

Bernanke, B. S., & Blinder, A. S. (1992). The Federal Funds Rate and the channels of monetary transmission. *American Economic Review, 82*(4), 901–921.

Bernanke, B. S., & Kuttner, K. N. (2005). What explains the stock market's reaction to Federal Reserve Policy? *Journal of Finance, 60*(3), 1221–1257.

Bernanke, B. S., & Mihov, I. (1998). Measuring monetary policy. *Quarterly Journal of Economics, 113*(3), 869–902.

Boyd, J. H., Hu, J., & Jagannathan, R. (2005). The stock market's reaction to unemployment news: Why bad news is usually good for stocks. *Journal of Finance, 60*(2), 649–672.

Campbell, J. R., Evans, C. L., Fisher, J. D., & Justiniano, A. (2012). Macroeconomic effects of the federal reserve forward guidance. *Brookings Papers on Economic Activity, 42*(1), 1–80.

Champagne, J., & Sekkel, R. (2018). Changes in monetary regimes and the identification of monetary policy shocks: Narrative evidence from Canada. *Journal of Monetary Economics, 99*(1), 72–87.

Chang, P.-L., & Sakata, S. (2007). Estimation of impulse response functions using long autoregression. *The Econometrics Journal, 10*(2), 453–469.

Christiano, L. J., Eichenbaum, M., & Evans, C. (1996). The effects of monetary policy shocks: Evidence from the flow of funds. *Review of Economics and Stastics, 78*(1), 16–34.

Christiano, L. J., Eichenbaum, M., & Evans, L. C. (1999). Monetary policy shocks: What have we learned and to what end? In *Handbook of macroeconomics* (Vols. 1, Part A, pp. 65–148).

Cloyne, J., & Hürtgen, P. (2016). The macroeconomic effects of monetary policy: A new measure for the United Kingdom. *American Economic Journal: Macroeconomics, 8*(4), 75–102.

Cochrane, J. H., & Piazzesi, M. (2002). The fed and interest rates - A high-frequency identification. *American Economic Review, 92*(2), 90–95.

Cochrane, J. H., & Piazzesi, M. (2005). Bond Risk Premia. *American Economic Review, 95*(1), 138–160.

Coibion, O. (2012). Are the effects of monetary policy shocks big or small? *American Economic Journal: Macroeconomics, 4*(2), 1–32.

Davies, H. (2014). *The financial crisis: Who is to blame* (1st ed.). Wiley.

Dedola, L., & Lippi, F. (2005). The monetary transmission mechanism: Evidence from the industries of five OECD countries. *European Economic Review, 49*(6), 1543–1569.

Dornbusch, R. (1976). Expectations and exchange rate dynamics. *Journal of Political Economy, 84*(6), 1161–1176.
Eichenbaum, M. (1992). Interpreting the macroeconomic time series facts: The effects of monetary policy': By Christopher Sims. *European Economic Review, 36*(5), 1001–1011.
Fama, E. F., & Bliss, R. R. (1987). The information in long-maturity forward rates. *American Economic Review, 77*(4), 680–692.
Faust, J., Swanson, E. T., & Wright, J. H. (2004). Identifying VARS based on high frequency futures data. *Journal of Monetary Economics, 51*(1), 1107–1131.
Friedman, M., & Schwartz, A. J. (1963). *A Monetary history of the United States, 1867–1960* (National Bureau of Economic Research Publications ed.). Princeton University Press.
Fry, R., & Pagan, A. (2011). Sign restrictions in structural vector autoregression: A critical review. *Journal of Economic Literature, 49*(4), 938–960.
Gertler, M., & Karadi, P. (2015). Monetary policy surprises, credit costs, and economic activity. *American Economic Journal: Macroeconomics, 7*(1), 44–76.
Gürkaynak, R. S., Sack, B., & Swanson, E. (2005a). Do actions speak louder than words? The response of asset prices to monetary policy actions and statements. *International Journal of Central Banking, 1*(1), 55–93.
Gürkaynak, R. S., Sack, B., & Swanson, E. T. (2005b). The sensitivity of long-term interest rates to economics news: Evidence and implications for macroeconomic models. *American Economic Review, 95*(1), 425–436.
Hamilton, J. D. (2008). Daily monetary shocks and new home sales. *Journal of Monetary Economics, 55*(7), 1171–1190.
Jarociński, M., & Karadi, P. (2020). Deconstructing monetary policy surprises—The role of information shocks. *American Economic Journal: Macroeconomics, 12*(2), 1–43.
Jordà, O. (2005). Estimation and inference of impulse responses by local projections. *American Economic Review, 95*(1), 161–182.
Kuttner, K. N. (2001). Monetary policy surprises and interest rates: Evidence from the Fed funds futures market. *Journal of Monetary Economics, 47*(3), 523–544.
Lucas, R. (1980). Equilibrium in a pure currency economy. *Economic Inquiry, 18*(2), 203–220.
Lucca, D. O., & Moench, E. (2015). The pre-FOMC announcement drift. *The Journal of Finance, 70*(1), 329–371.
Marcellino, M., Stock, J. H., & Watson, M. W. (2006). A comparison of direct and iterated mul tistep AR methods for forecasting macroeconomic time series. *Journal of Econometrics, 135*(1 2), 499 526.
Miranda-Agrippino, S., & Ricco, G. (2021). The transmission of monetary policy shocks. *American Economic Journal: Macroeconomics, 13*(3), 74–107.
Mountford, A. (2005). Leaning into the wind: A structural VAR investigation of the UK monetary policy. *Oxford Bulletin of Economics and Statistics, 67*(5), 597–621.
Murgia, L. M. (2020). The effects of monetary policy shocks on macroeconomic variables: Evidence from the Eurozone. *Economics Letters, 186*(1), 1–4.
Newey, W., & West, K. (1987). A simple, positive semi-definite, heteroskedasticity and atucorrelation consistent covariance matrix. *Econometrica, 55*(3), 703–708.
Piazzesi, M., & Swanson, E. T. (2008). Futures prices as risk-adjusted forecasts of monetary policy. *Journal of Monetary Economics, 55*(4), 677–691.
Plagborg-Møller, M., & Wolf, C. K. (2021). Local projections and VARs estimate the same impulse responses. *Econometrica, 89*(2), 955–980.
Rafiq, M., & Mallick, S. (2008). The effect of monetary policy on output in EMU3: A sign restrictions approach. *Journal of Macroeconomics, 30*(1), 1756–1791.
Ramey, V. A. (2016). Macroeconomic shocks and their propagation. In *Handbook of macroeconomics* (pp. 71–162). Elsevier.
Reichilin, L. (2023). *"A FED of our times", a review essay on twentieth century monetary policy by Ben Bernanke*. CEPR discussion paper (1–23).

Romer, C. D., & Romer, D. H. (1989). Does monetary policy matter? A new test in the Spirit of Friedman and Schwartz. In O. Fischer (Ed.), *NBER macroeconomics annual 1989, Volume 4* (pp. 121–184). MIT Press.

Romer, C., & Romer, D. H. (2000). Federal Reserve Information and the behavior of interest rates. *American Economic Review, 9*(3), 429–457.

Romer, C. D., & Romer, D. H. (2004). A new measure of monetary shocks: Derivation and implications. *American Economic Review, 94*(4), 1055–1084.

Romer, C. D., & Romer, D. H. (2023). Presidential address: Does monetary policy matter? The narrative approach after 35 years. *American Economic Review, 113*(6), 1395–1423.

Rudebusch, G. D. (1998). Do measures of monetary policy in a Var make sense? *International Economic Review, 39*(4), 907–931.

Scholl, A., & Uhlig, H. (2008). New evidence on the puzzles: Results from agnostic identification on monetary policy and exchange rates. *Journal of International Economics, 76*(1), 1–13.

Sims, C. A. (1980). Macroeconomics and reality. *Econometrica, 48*(1), 1–48.

Sims, C. A. (1992). Interpreting the macroeconomic time series facts: The effects of monetary policy. *European Economic Review, 35*(6), 975–1000.

Svensson, L. E. (2003). What is wrong with Taylor rules? Using judgment in monetary policy through targeting rules. *Journal of Economic Literature, 41*(2), 426–477.

Uhlig, H. (2005). What are the effects of monetary policy on output? Results from an agnostic identification procedure. *Journal of Monetary Economics, 52*(1), 381–419.

Chapter 6
Estimating Monetary Policy Shocks: Data and Practical Aspects

6.1 Introduction

Alex Edmans' study "*Learning from a 1000 Rejections*" lists several factors that persuade a journal editor to reject a submitted working paper. In first place we find (naturally) the paper's contribution to the extant academic field. Next, is how the study is executed. As a postdoctoral student, finding a gap in the literature and a valuable contribution is challenging. A further difficult task is how to turn research ideas into a properly "executed" paper, whether into a theoretical model or into an empirical framework. Particularly when designing an empirical research, clarity on the theoretical background is essential (i.e., key literature references as well as their modelling approaches), followed by steps to tackle the research's practical aspects.

For a young scholar, a suitable way to enter a research field and learn how to complete a paper is simply to backtest and replicate results of the literature milestone papers (Kohler & Cortina, 2019). Interestingly, that way of performing a research program has become simpler in recent times, as most journals require authors to upload both data and programming codes. However, when a researcher is in the initial steps of a research program, it could be difficult to compile a full list of the papers that provided fundamental contributions in that stream of literature. Additionally, and on the practical side, when learning how to use a new software package, tips and hints can be very precious and support the researcher in saving time and effort.

This chapter is designed to present guidelines and equip young scholars to be able to reproduce and extend the results of the seminal papers that I reviewed in Chap. 5. I provide a few examples of replication procedures and suggest a comprehensive list of references that are part of the vast literature that has been analysing monetary policy shocks and their effects on macroeconomic and financial market variables. Those references include useful links to IT resources that are essential to redo most empirical analyses and backtest original results. In the end, my goal is to

L. M. Murgia, *The Impact of Monetary Policy*, Financial and Monetary Policy Studies 56, https://doi.org/10.1007/978-3-032-15451-4_6

pave the way for the work required to replicate past empirical findings and suggest basic guidelines to young scholars approaching their first steps into the monetary policy shock field of research.

In the financial economics stream of literature, three different coding tools were mainstream: R, Stata, and Matlab. More recently Python has earned a vast popularity for its computational tools and availability to use for machine learning tasks. Most of the studies presented in Chap. 5 were developed in either R or Matlab. The present chapter will focus on the usage of R for two main reasons: (1) it is freely available to everyone; (2) it is highly extensible through user-created packages, backed by a vibrant community of developers.

What differentiates the examples presented in this chapter from most other examples available online and in book format is the fact that we do not focus on single packages, but rather provide a comprehensive overview of all the passages required to perform an empirical analysis (from loading data into the software, to performing regressions, and ultimately exporting results and graphs). Background related to theoretical econometrics models discussed in Chap. 5 (e.g., vector autoregressive models) is prerequisite and will be taken for granted. I will also discuss the practical implementation of time series analyses.[1]

6.2 R Packages and Examples of Implementation

In this section I illustrate some exercises executed with R, the most used econometrics package in research on monetary policy shocks and macroeconomic variables. Data and code that run the exercises that I illustrate hereby are available in the online material package.

I start with a simple example that employs European data to execute a narrative shock series like in Romer and Romer (2004). The time series data are from year 2000 through 2023: a period that surrounds the Covid-19 pandemic crisis in years 2020 and 2021 and the accompanying macroeconomic shock.

The next example I present makes use of high-frequency data, to illustrate a shock time series as in Kerssenfischer (2022). That example shows the effects of monetary shocks on financial markets and macroeconomic variables.

However, even though the primary motivation to present those examples is to illustrate to junior readers how to design econometrics methods when researching monetary policy shocks, an additional objective is to present some fresh results in the field that take advantage of a longer time series which surrounds the economic consequences of the Covid-19 pandemic shock.

[1] For a comprehensive theoretical review of the models and general R application see Pfaff (2008).

6.2.1 Developing a Narrative Shock Series for Europe

The first example that uses Eurozone data shows the comparison between two identification strategies largely discussed in Chap. 5. The first strategy utilizes an updated version of the narrative time series presented by Murgia (2020). That study exploits the approach and methodologies developed in Romer and Romer (2004), Cloyne and Hürtgen (2016), and Champagne and Sekkel (2018).

The time series data is from 2000 to 2023, which includes the two years that surround the COVID-19 shock. The adopted econometric model follows the first stage VAR of Romer and Romer (2004), as illustrated in Chap. 5. However, as in Murgia (2020), I extend Romer and Romer's (2004) baseline equation by including further explanatory variables, as proposed in Cloyne and Hürtgen (2016) and Champagne and Sekkel (2018). Further controls I add to the shock series are the Eurostoxx 50 stock index ($EU50_{m0}$), the binary exchange rate EURUSD (EX_{m0}), and the Effective Federal Funds Rate Level.

The resulting estimated model is shown below in Eq. (6.1):

$$\Delta ff_m = \alpha + \beta\, ffb_{m-14} + \sum_{i=-1}^{2} \gamma_i \widetilde{y_{mi}} + \sum_{i=-1}^{2} \delta_i \widetilde{(y_{mi} - y_{m-1,i})}$$

$$+ \sum_{i=-1}^{2} \varphi_i \widetilde{\pi_{mi}} + \sum_{i=-1}^{2} \theta_i \widetilde{(\pi_{mi} - \pi_{m-1,i})} + \rho \widetilde{u_{m0}} + EU50_m$$

$$+ \tau EX_m + \chi FFR_m + \omega TA_m + {}_m \tag{6.1}$$

The definitions for variables in Eq. (6.1) are detailed in Table 6.1.

To perform a first stage vector autoregressive regression through R, the "vars" package is needed. To install the package, we follow the command[2]:

Table 6.1 Variables in Eq. (6.1)

Symbol	Name
Δff_m	Interest rate changes
ffb_{m-14}	Interest rate level two weeks prior to the meeting
Δy_{mi}	Inflation forecast
$\tilde{\pi}_{mi}$	GDP forecast
$\tilde{u}_{m0}$	Last available unemployment rate
$EU50_{m0}$	Eurostoxx 50 Index level at the meeting date
EX_{m0}	EURUSD exchange rate level at the meeting date
FFR_{m0}	Federal Funds Target Rate level at the meeting date
TA_m	Total Assets of the ECB at the meeting date

[2] The documentation and summary of function can be found at: https://www.rdocumentation.org/packages/vars/versions/1.6-0 or on the personal website of the maintainer that contains other relevant resources: https://www.pfaffikus.de/. The PDF manual can be found at: https://www.pfaffikus.de/rpacks/vars/files/manual-vars.pdf.

```
install.packages('vars') #1
```

when installing from CRAN, however, packages can also be available on R-Forge and GitHub. Next, we need to load the package:

```
library(vars) #1
```

The package contains a dataset useful for practicing VAR models. It is stored in MS Office Excel files that must be re-loaded into the R space to be used.

Box 6.1 First Time User Tip!
Make sure that you save the excel file in a specific folder and you set the working directory to be that folder! To set the working directory follow the command "Change dir…" that can be found in "File" tab.

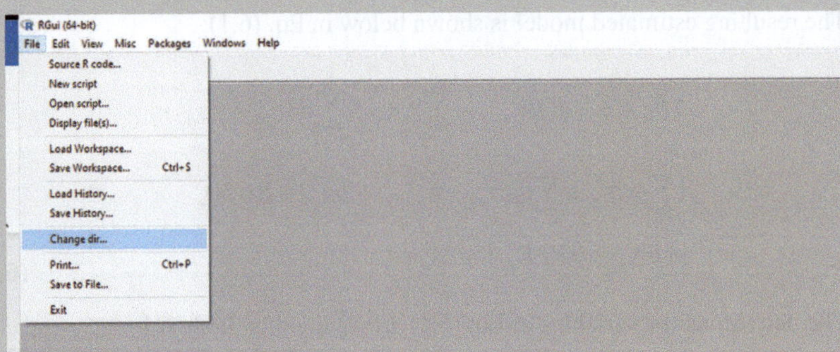

To do the re-loading into the R space, we can use the package command "readxl"[3]:

```
install.packages('readxl') #1
library(readxl) #2
```

And since the file is saved in.xlsx format, the reference function is:

```
data_ECB <- read_xlsx("Yourfile.xlsx","Spreadsheet_Name")
```

is the excel spreadsheet name. Without specifying the name of the excel spreadsheet, R will simply include the first available one.

If we call the name of the dataset in the R console, we will obtain a preview of the dataset as shown in the next Fig. 6.1:

[3] The cran documentation can be found: https://cran.r-project.org/web/packages/readxl/index.html

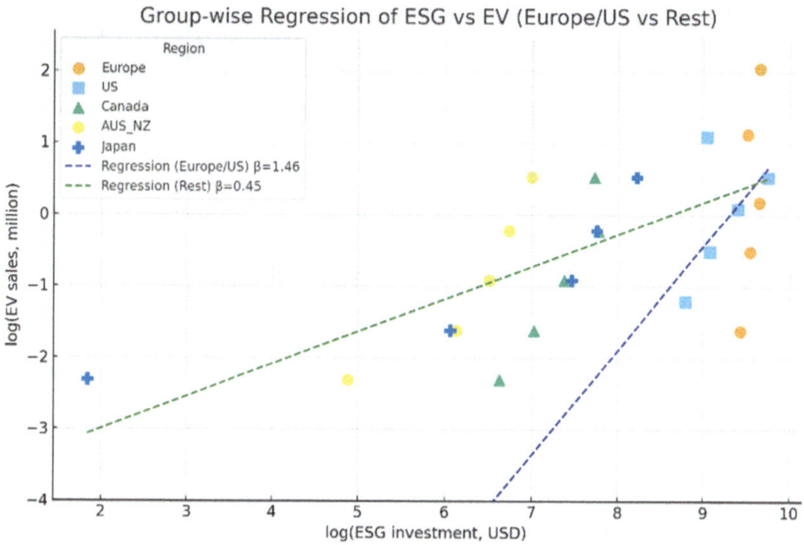

Fig. 6.1 R console. The figure shows an example of a dataset shown in the R console. Source: Author's Computation

After loading the dataset, we can extract the variables to be used in the analysis. Next, ask R to list them, to check we are using the right ones:

```
>names (data_ECB)
```

We can extract and rename the variables. We can assign a new name to variables, linking it to the dataset name and the dataset variable name, as in the following example:

```
>time_ECB=data_ECB$Date #1
>target_rate_change_ECB=data_ECB$Target_Rate_Change_FRED #2
```

"time_ECB" is the variable that includes the dates of the ECB meeting, whereas "target_rate_change_ECB" contains the changes in the Marginal Rate of Operations interest rates of the ECB.

After loading all the necessary variables, we need to construct a matrix to run the first stage VAR.

```
>ECB=(as.matrix(cbind(all the variables that you wish to include
in the VAR, see table 6.1)))
```

This is the set of variables required to estimate Eq. (6.1), and is the last step before running the VAR analysis using the package function "VAR".

```
>model_1_ECB=VAR(ECB,p=1,type="both") #1
>summary(model_1_ECB, equation="target_rate_change_ECB") #2
```

The first line of coding specifies the VAR model using the matrix of variables "ECB". The second line calls out the results for the VAR related to the "target_rate_change_ECB" as the dependent variable.

As in Murgia (2020), the purpose of this first step is to extract the residuals of Eq. (6.1). First stage VAR estimates have important implications for explaining the policymakers' decisions, which in this exercise are those of the ECB Governing Council. Table 6.2 shows results of the first stage VARs, adding VARs that reproduce the original Romer and Romer (2004) equation in the same period.

It is worth noting that Table 6.2 contains results that go behind the econometric exercise, and present novel estimates with data surrounding the pandemic period. The comparison with Romer and Romer (2004) is relatively straightforward. The R^2 suggest that the extended model proposed in Murgia (2020) has more explanatory power, given the inclusion of the additional variables. What is particularly interesting, and was found also by Champagne and Sekkel (2018) in the case of Canada, is

Table 6.2 First stage VAR

	Romer and Romer (2004)		Extended Murgia (2020)	
	Coeff	SE	Coeff	SE
Δ Interest Rate	0.209	0.064	0.018	0.068
Output				
Forecast (1y)	−0.013	0.009	−0.016	0.008
Forecast (2y)	0.071	0.026	0.040	0.029
Forecast Δ (1y)	0.005	0.009	0.008	0.008
Forecast Δ (2y)	−0.031	0.051	−0.014	0.019
Inflation				
Forecast (1y)	0.051	0.024	0.093	0.025
Forecast (2y)	0.124	0.065	0.049	0.063
Forecast Δ (1y)	0.102	0.052	0.073	0.050
Forecast Δ (2y)	−0.116	0.109	−0.083	0.101
Macro variables				
Unemployment Rate	0.002	0.009	0.011	0.009
Interest Rate$_{(t-14)}$	−0.034	0.014	−0.076	0.015
Total Assets			−0.000	0.001
Market variables				
Eurostoxx 50 Level			0.001	0.001
EFF Rate			0.047	0.011
EURUSD Ex Rate			0.000	0.001
Observations	243		243	
R^2	0.337		0.433	
Adjusted R^2	0.303		0.393	

Notes: The column "Coeff" presents the coefficients and "SE" presents the robust standard errors.

the importance of the Effective Federal Funds rate (Eff Rate). The variable is, in fact, positive and statistically significant, suggesting the influence of FED policy on ECB decisions.

I adopt the package "stargazer"[4] to export table results from the R package to Word software (MS@)[5]

```
install.packages('stargazer') #1
stargazer(model_1_ECB$varresult$target_rate_change_
ECB,type="text",
title="VAR Model - ECB ",
digits=3, align=TRUE, out="var_1_ECB.doc") #2
```

The first line of code is to install the packages. The second line is the stargazer function, and the model to be exported is specified in text form. Following are different preferences to frame the layout of the exported table. It is important to specify the format in which we wish to export our results in the option "out". In this case the export is done in Word format file (.doc); however, it can also be exported in alternative formats (e.g., ".txt", ".csv").

Box 6.2 First Time User Tip!
Any exported file from R, will be automatically saved in the chosen working directory that we have set at the beginning of the exercise.

The next step is to extract the model residuals to employ them as our shock series in the two-stage least squares analysis. Extracting the residuals from any equation in R is straightforward with the option "residuals" when analysing regression results.

```
ECB_monetary_shocks=residuals(model_1_ECB)
```

Model residuals are re-named "ECB_monetary_shocks" and the shock series is stored in a variable that contains all residuals from VAR least squares models. It is important to recall that a first step when analysing monetary shocks is to source data at a meeting-by-meeting frequency. Differently, explanatory macroeconomic variables are only available at monthly frequency. As done in past papers, we also assign 0% shock to all "missing months".

[4]The documentation can be found: https://www.rdocumentation.org/packages/stargazer/versions/5.2.3/topics/stargazer

Additional useful material is made available at: https://libguides.princeton.edu/R-stargazer.

[5]The documentation can be found: https://www.rdocumentation.org/packages/stargazer/versions/5.2.3/topics/stargazer

Additional useful material is made available at: https://libguides.princeton.edu/R-stargazer.

First, we store the shock series in a "csv" file, reload it into R, and extract the residuals only referring to the equation of the interest rate changes.

```
write.csv(ECB_monetary_shocks,file="monetary_shocks_ECB.csv",
quote=F,na='NA', row.names=T) #1

monetary_shocks_ECB<-read.csv(file="monetary_shocks_ECB.csv") #2
monetary_shocks_ECB=monetary_shocks_ECB$target_rate_change_ECB
```

The functions "write.csv" and "read.csv" are all part of the "readxl" package loaded when the exercise starts. Once the initial dataset is loaded, we can easily extract the variable following similar commands. We could also add to the analysis a useful graph which plots the shock series and long-term interest rate changes.

```
#plotting monetary shocks with also target interest rate change
plot(time_ECB_1,monetary_shocks_ECB,type='l',lty=1,lwd=2,
col="red",xlab="Sample Period - (2000-2023)",
ylab="%",main="Exogenous Monetary Shocks - ECB") #1
par(new='true') #2
plot(target_rate_change_ECB,type="l",lty=2,
lwd=1,col="black",xlab="",ylab="",xaxt="n",yaxt="n") #3
par(new='true') #4
legend(x="bottomright",y="-2.000",legend = c("Monetary
Shocks","Target Rate Changes"),
 col=c("red","black"),pch = c("","","")) #5
```

The presented code includes 2 different time series: the first is our series of monetary shocks, and the second has the changes in interest rates. The code's last line presents how to include a simple legend at the bottom of the figure. Lines 2 and 4 include the code to plot multiple time series within the same graph in R. Figure 6.2 displays the code's graphical representation.

At first glance, looking at the data pattern before the 2008 financial crisis, it is apparent that the two series of shocks (red and green line) had a very close co-movement, with just a hint of anticipation from the "Extended Murgia (2020)". The two series of shocks start to diverge from each other when the financial crisis comes out. However, it also appears that the "Extended Murgia (2020)" was anticipating the imminent cut to interest rates.

Useful Exercises

- Control for crisis period during the time series using the NBER recession dummy. https://fred.stlouisfed.org/series/USREC
- Include and exclude crisis period from the sample.

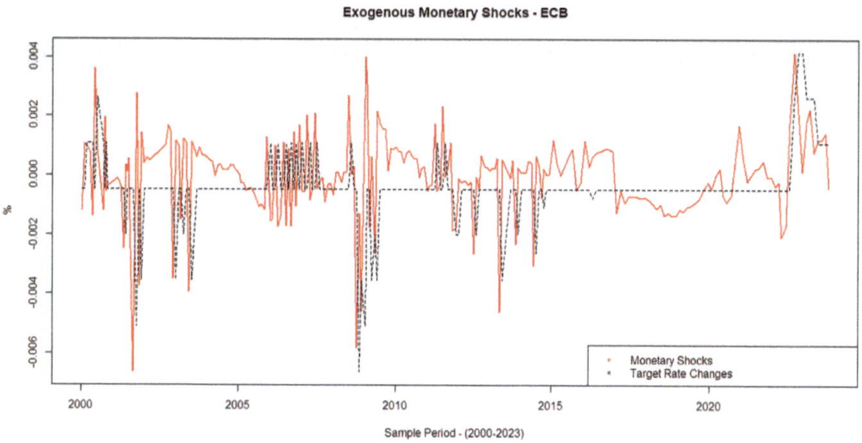

Fig. 6.2 Exogenous monetary shocks—ECB. The figure presents the shock series computed extracting the residuals from Eq. (6.1). Along with the shock series we plot the series of the target interest rate. Source: Author's Computations

6.2.2 *The Shock Series Effects on Macroeconomic Variables*

As a second exercise with the R package I propose to analyse the effects of monetary policy shocks on macroeconomic variables taking advantage of the previous application output that developed a shock time series. The focus here is on assessing the effect of shocks on price levels (approximated by the HCPI All Items Eurozone index, a proxy for Eurozone inflation) and economic output (approximated by the Eurozone unemployment rate).[6] In recent studies (e.g., Romer & Romer, 2023) the Jorda (2005) methodology became frequently adopted. Jorda (2005) local linear projections were substantially discussed in Chap. 5, as an easier and precise methodology to estimate impulse responses.

I estimate the following regression model:

$$x_{t+h} - x_t = c + \varphi_h(L) z_{t-1} + \beta_h m_t + \varepsilon_{t+h} \tag{6.2}$$

where $h = 0,1,2,\ldots 24$. The variable of interest is x, $\varphi_h(L)$ is a polynomial lag operator, z_{t-1} is a vector of controls, and m_t is the measure of monetary policy shocks.

Before entering into the code details, there are some technical steps that need to be discussed, as they are standard approaches in the literature. The shock series estimated is at a meeting-by-meeting frequency and needs to be converted into a monthly shock series. As in most of the literature, the shock series is converted to monthly by simply assigning "0" to the months without a meeting. Additionally,

[6] Data description is included in the online package.

since the variables for this model are "level" variables, the shock series is cumulated. To estimate the local linear projections model we need to install and load a new R package:

```
install.packages('lpirfs') #1[7]
library(lpirfs) #2
```

To load the data into R previous exercise steps can be re-used.

Box 6.3 First Time User Tip!
With the package lpirfs the data as to be grouped in a "Data frame" rather than in a matrix.

The previous code can be used with this addition:

```
macro=as.matrix(cbind(inflation,unemployment,commodit
y,SHOCKS))
macro=as.data.frame(macro)
```

The function that allows us to run the model is "lp_lin". The code shown here does not produce the impulse responses. However, it allows us to plot the impulse responses on the variable of interest. In the current exercise, we run a simple model, following past work parameters[8] and using an "external shock".

```
lp_eu=lp_lin(macro,                                  #1
lags_endog_lin=24,                                   #2
shock_type= SHOCKS,                                  #3
confint=1.96,                        #4
trend=0,                                  #5
hor=24)                               #6
```

For the plots the following packages are also needed:

[7]A comprehensive guide and example on the use of the package can be found at https://journal.r-project.org/archive/2019/RJ-2019-052/RJ-2019-052.pdf.

[8]We use 24 lags as in Cloyne and Hürtgen (2016) and the example of Jorda's (2005) paper from ?????

```
library(dplyr)[9]                  #1
library(gridExtra)[10]           #2
library(ggpubr)[11]                 #3
```

To plot the graphs we employ the plot_lin function, specifically as part of this package.

```
eu_plot<-plot_lin(lp_eu) #1
eu_plot_all<-sapply(eu_plot, ggplotGrob) #2
marrangeGrob(eu_plot_all, nrow = 4, ncol = 4,top = NULL) #3
```

In coding I first create the plots (#1), next I formulate a "grob" object (#2), which combines the multiple impulse responses that have been estimated through the model. Then I arrange the "grob" objects on a single page, in 4 rows (nrow) and 4 columns (ncol).

The output of the code is illustrated in the following Fig. 6.3.

This figure shows the effect of each variable on each other, as we would have with a VAR. However, I'm also interested in the impact of the monetary shock series "SHOCKS" on inflation and unemployment, which are the bottom left figures. Even though the graphs are accurate, they might not be ideal to be inserted into the final draft of a working paper.

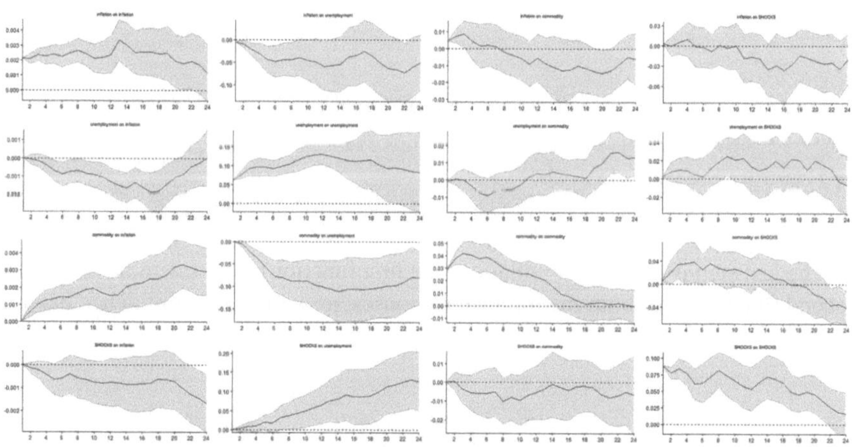

Fig. 6.3 Full local projections output. The figure includes the full output of model 6.2 for all the variables. The first row includes the effect of inflation on all the other variables. The second row includes the effect of unemployment on all the other variables. The third row includes the effect of the commodity index on all the variables. Lastly, the fourth line includes the effect of our measure of shocks on all the other variables. Source: Authors Computations

[9] https://cran.r-project.org/web/packages/dplyr/readme/README.html

[10] https://cran.r-project.org/web/packages/gridExtra/index.html

[11] https://cran.r-project.org/web/packages/ggpubr/index.html

We can extract the impulse response functions and the confidence intervals to further plot them in more tailored figures. To extract the functions we go back to our "lp_eu" model. We need to extract the first two functions of the 4th variable in the model, therefore:

```
mps_irf=lp_eu$irf_lin_mean[,,4]                         #1
mps_irf=as.data.frame(mps_irf)                           #2
mps_irf=(t(mps_irf))                                           #3
mps_irf=as.data.frame(cbind(mps_irf[,1],mps_
irf[,2]))             #4
```

In #1 we extract all the impulse responses ("irf_lin_mean") from the 4th variable, name it as a data frame and transpose into column vectors. Lastly, we only keep the first and the second functions that refer to inflation and unemployment.

The same procedure is followed to extract the low confidence band ("irf_lin_low") and the high ("irf_lin_up") confidence band.

```
#Low Confidence Interval
mps_irf_low=lp_eu$irf_lin_low[,,4] #1
mps_irf_low=as.data.frame(mps_irf_low) #2
mps_irf_low=(t(mps_irf_low)) #3
mps_irf_low=as.data.frame(cbind(mps_irf_low[,1],mps_irf_
low[,2])) #4

#High Confidence Interval
mps_irf_up=lp_eu$irf_lin_up[,,4] #1
mps_irf_up=as.data.frame(mps_irf_up) #2
mps_irf_up=(t(mps_irf_up)) #3
mps_irf_up=as.data.frame(cbind(mps_irf_up[,1],mps_irf_up[,2])) #4
```

The last step is to separate inflation (the first function) from unemployment (the second function), for both the impulse responses, as well as the confidence bands.

```
#EXTRACTING THE SINGLE FUNCTIONS
#IRF
infl_eu_1=c(mps_irf[,1])                        #1 prices
ur_eu_1=c(mps_irf[,2])                            #2 output
#CI
infl_eu_up=c(mps_irf_up[,1])                #3
infl_eu_low=c(mps_irf_low[,1])            #4
ur_eu_up=c(mps_irf_up[,2])                      #5
ur_eu_low=c(mps_irf_low[,2])                  #6
```

After this we have all the vector data to plot our separate figures.

Box 6.4 First Time User Tip!
We need an x-axis to plot the impulse responses functions over the time horizon that we have chosen in the model, which in this case was 24 periods ahead.

```
x_axis = c(1:25)
```

We can plot one graph at a time, as well as combine two different plots. In this case, we want to combine in one figure the two plots related to inflation and unemployment rate. The code that executes it has to be positioned before the plots:

```
par(mfrow=c(1,2),oma=c(2,0,2,0)) #1
```

This function is an easy way to combine different plots in R.[12]

Box 6.5 First Time User Tip!
The "par(mfrow)" function and the "layout" function are an easy way to arrange multiple different plots in R.

Further we can include the code to plot the impulse response function along with the confidence intervals. In this specific code, we prefer to plot the confidence intervals as a grey area around the graph rather than a line.

[12] More details on this function and arranging plots in R can be found: https://bookdown.org/ndphillips/YaRrr/arranging-plots-with-parmfrow-and-layout.html

```
#inflation plot
plot(x_axis,infl_eu_1,type
="n",                                                     #1
ylim=c(-0.005,0.005),                      #2
xlim=c(min(x_axis),max(x_axis)),                      #3
ylab="%",                                      #4
xlab="Months",                                          #5
main="Panel A: Inflation",cex.lab=1,cex.axis=1,cex.main=1)  #6
polygon(                   #7

c(1:length(infl_eu_up), length(infl_eu_
low):1),                      #8
 c(infl_eu_up, rev(infl_eu_low)),                          #9
 col = "grey90", border = NA)                          #10
lines(infl_eu_1,col="blue",
lwd=1)                                                     #11
points(infl_eu_1,type="p",pch=20,col="b
lue")                              #12
abline(h=0,col="red")                                              #13

#unemployment rate plot
plot(x_axis,ur_eu_1,type
="n",                                        #1
xlim=c(min(x_axis),max(x_
axis)),                                                      #2
ylim=c(0,0.25),                                           #3
ylab="%",                                  #4
xlab="Months",                                           #5
main="Panel B: Unemployment",cex.lab=1,cex.axis=1,cex.main=1)  #6
polygon(                   #7

c(1:length(ur_eu_up), length(ur_eu_low):1),                     #8

c(ur_eu_up, rev(ur_eu_
low)),                                                     #9
 col = "grey90", border =
NA)                                           #10
lines(ur_eu_1,col="blue",
lwd=1)                                         #11
points(ur_eu_1,type="p",pch=20,col="b
lue")                          #12
abline(h=0,col="red")                                     #13
```

Both graphs follow the same structure. Variable definitions are included (x-axis and y-axis). In lines 2 and 3 we define the limit of the axis; with the y-axis, it is

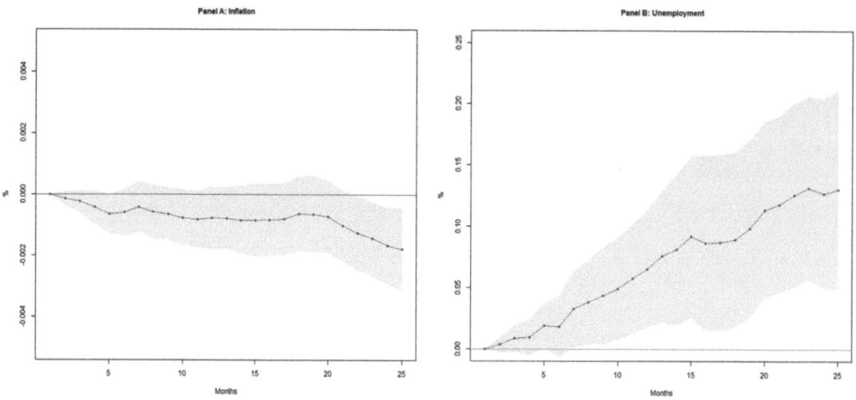

Fig. 6.4 Local projection output for prices and output. The figure presents an extraction of Fig. 6.3, where only the effects of "SHOCKS" on Inflation and unemployment are considered. Source: Author's Computations

perhaps easier to include the limits manually since the maximum and minimum as in the x-axis case might distort excessively the plot graphics. In line 4 and 5 we include the labels of the axis, followed by the title ("main") and the dimensions of the included text.

To plot the confidence interval in the form of an area we plot a polygon (from line 7 to 10), giving the length and the dimension as well as the shades of colour.[13] Lastly, we define the width and colour of the lines, as well as the above points. Data points can be very useful in this type of graph to better appreciate the magnitude at which macro variables change direction. The last element is a horizontal red line (#13) to highlight 0 and facilitate the interpretation of the results and their statistical significance. Code final graphs are shown in Fig. 6.4.

The functions show that inflation drops mildly after 20 months from a 100 basis points shocks. Unemployment, on the other hand, raises and it is statistically significant from 6 months after the shock.

Useful Exercises

- Control the robustness of the exercise by changing the lags level.
- Analyse the response across different periods and with different confidence bands. Plot multiple confidence bands in the extracted graphs.

[13] For a comprehensive R colour cheat sheet see: https://www.nceas.ucsb.edu/sites/default/files/2020-04/colorPaletteCheatsheet.pdf

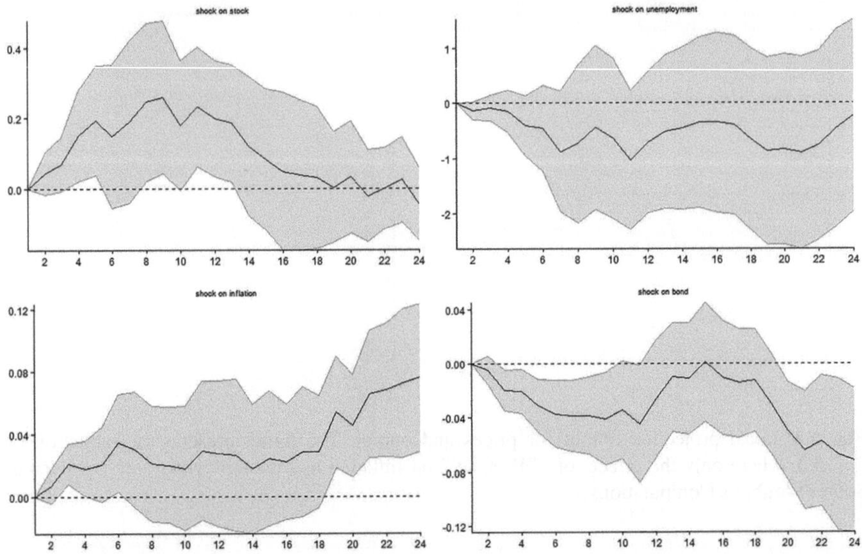

Fig. 6.5 MK series analysis. The figure represents an extraction of the output of model 6.2, when the shock series is represented by the series of Kerssenfischer (2022). The effect of the HF shock series is shown on stocks, inflation, unemployment and a Eurozone Investment Grade Bond index. Source: Author's Computations

6.2.3 High-Frequency Evidence

Given the increasing popularity of methods and the availability of high-frequency data, I briefly illustrate the effects that a high-frequency monetary shock series could have on financial markets. Specifically, I re-run the local linear projection model presented in Eq. (6.2) against five variables. My model includes inflation, unemployment, the commodity index from the previous var, the *log* of the Eurostoxx 50 index, and the *log* of the FTSE Euro Broad Investment Grade Bond Index. Shock series are taken from the work of Kerssenfischer (2022),[14] who computes them as the immediate change in 2-year German bond yields. We employ the extended version until June 2023 (the series employed in the published work stops in 2019, and therefore doesn't include the pandemic period). Kerssenfischer (2022) does not find any effect on the stock market and economic expectations, whereas a strong effect is found on exchange rates and interest rates yields. Moreover, consistent with extant literature (Jarociński & Karadi, 2020), the shock series is next split between "pure shocks" and "information shocks". Kerssenfischer (2022), however, obtains results that are broadly aligned with available evidence.

[14] We thank Mark Kerssenfischer for generously sharing his work, available on his personal website https://sites.google.com/site/markkerssenfischer.

Table 6.3 Monetary policy shocks and their effect on output and prices

References	DOI	Methodology	Sample Period	IT resource available
Christiano et al. (1999)	https://doi.org/10.1016/S1574-0048(99)01005-8	SVAR	1965–1995	Tutorial: Structural Vector Autoregression Models by Kevin Kotzé https://kevinkotze.github.io/ts-8-tut/ svars: An R Package for Data-Driven Identification in Multivariate Time Series Analysis https://cran.r-project.org/web/packages/svars/vignettes/svars.pdf
Faust et al. (2004)		HFI—using close—to—close federal funds futures rates. SVAR methodology for impulse responses from Christiano et al. (1999)	1991–2001	
Romer and Romer (2004)	DOI: 10.1257/000282804200265	Narrative methodology	1969–1996	Original Replication package available at: https://www.openicpsr.org/openicpsr/project/116025/version/V1/view Updated Shocks: https://www.openicpsr.org/openicpsr/project/135741/version/V1/view;jsessionid=CF9FCE42C4A34EB62299C655CE71F2F9 FOMC dates scraps: https://www.r-bloggers.com/2015/01/fomc-dates-full-history-web-scrape/
Jorda (2005)	DOI: 10.1257/000282805382851 8	Local Linear Projections	NA	Original Replication package available at: https://www.openicpsr.org/openicpsr/project/116037/version/V1/view R resources: "lpirfs: An R Package to Estimate Impulse Response Functions by Local Projections" by Philipp Adämmer. https://journal.r-project.org/archive/2019/RJ-2019-052/RJ-2019-052.pdf Example: https://adaemmerp.github.io/lpirfs/README_docs.html R code to calculate and plot impulse responses from local projections https://github.com/stefanangrick/local-projections

(continued)

Table 6.3 (continued)

References	DOI	Methodology	Sample Period	IT resource available
Uhlig (2005)	https://doi.org/10.1016/j.jmoneco.2004.05.007	SVAR with sign-restrictions.		svars: An R Package for Data-Driven Identification in Multivariate Time Series Analysis https://cran.r-project.org/web/packages/svars/vignettes/svars.pdf
Bernanke et al. (2005)	https://doi.org/10.1162/0033553053327452	FAVAR		Replication of the empirical results at: Luvsannyam and Batmunkh (2019) https://doi.org/10.1002/jae.2677 Data file: http://qed.econ.queensu.ca/jae/datasets/luvsannyam001/ R resources for replication: https://jbduarte.com/blog/time%20series/r/favar/2020/04/24/FAVAR-Replication.html https://rpubs.com/andresmtnezglez/738398 https://cran.r-project.org/web/packages/FAVAR/index.html
Coibion (2012)	DOI: 10.1257/mac.4.2.1	"Robust Romer and Romer (2004)"	1970–1996	Original Replication Package: https://www.openicpsr.org/openicpsr/project/114243/version/V1/view
Barakchian and Crowe (2013)	https://doi.org/10.1016/j.jmoneco.2013.09.006	HFI, Romer & Romer hybrid VAR	1988-2008	Data are analogous to the work of Kuttner (2001) and Romer and Romer (2004). For the VAR coding, see replication package of Romer and Romer (2004).
Gertler and Karadi (2015)	DOI: 10.1257/mac.20130329	HFI-Proxy SVAR	1979–2012	Original Replication Package: https://www.openicpsr.org/openicpsr/project/114082/version/V1/view
Cloyne and Hürtgen (2016)	DOI: 10.1257/mac.20150093	Narrative, Romer and Romer (2004) VAR, Local Projections Jorda (2005)	1975–2007	Original Replication Package: https://www.openicpsr.org/openicpsr/project/114114/version/V1/view
Champagne and Sekkel (2018)	https://doi.org/10.1016/j.jmoneco.2018.06.002	Narrative, Romer and Romer (2004) VAR, Local Projections Jorda (2005)	1974–2015	All available supplementary files in Appendix A: https://www.sciencedirect.com/science/article/pii/S0304393218303301

Altavilla et al. (2019)	https://doi.org/10.1016/j.jmoneco.2019.08.016	HFI data following Kuttner (2001) and QE identification from Swanson (2021), and OLS methodology for asset pricing responses.	2002–2018	Details of the database construction are presented in Appendices B, C, and D. The database is updated periodically and is available at https://www.ecb.europa.eu/pub/pdf/annex/Dataset_EA-MPD.xlsx. All available supplementary files in Appendix A: https://www.sciencedirect.com/science/article/pii/S0304393219301497#bib0025
Cesa-Bianchi et al. (2020)	https://doi.org/10.1016/j.euroecorev.2020.103375	HFI data following Kuttner (2001) and VAR.	1992–2015	All available supplementary files in Appendix C: https://www.sciencedirect.com/science/article/pii/S0014292120300076#sec0017
Jarociński and Karadi (2020)	DOI: 10.1257/mac.20180090	HFI data co-movements of interest rates and stock prices. SVAR for responses.	1990–2016	Original Replication Package: https://www.aeaweb.org/journals/dataset?id=10.1257/mac.20180090
Miranda-Agrippino and Ricco (2021)	DOI: 10.1257/mac.20180124	HFI and hybrid Romer and Romer (2004) VAR.	1979–2014	Original Replication Package: https://www.openicpsr.org/openicpsr/project/116841/version/V1/view Additional material from authors page: https://silviamirandaagrippino.com/code-data
Kerssenfischer (2022)	https://doi.org/10.1016/j.econlet.2022.110570	HFI data and sign-restriction methodology.	2022–2019	Replication files and shock series data available on: https://sites.google.com/site/markkerssenfischer
Bauer and Swanson (2023)	DOI: 10.1257/aer.20201220	HFI. Survey of Forecasters in the Blue Chip panel.	1995–2014	Original Replication Package: https://www.openicpsr.org/openicpsr/project/181661/version/V2/view

In Fig. 6.5[15] I present my analyses that exploit local linear projections instead of a VAR and that add commodity prices.

The impulse responses are run with 6 lags and plotted along with 90% confidence bands. I find contradictory results for the stock market and inflation. In both cases, results point to an increase in stock market returns as well as inflation: both results are opposite to theoretical predictions. The unique result consistent with theory is the effect on investment grade bond values, which drop instantaneously. The bond price impact shows that the identification results in the correct prediction for the fixed income market. Kerssenfischer (2022) results are similar. In a second step analysis he finds that only when separating pure from information shocks, following a sign-restriction methodology, his results are consistent with theory (Uhlig, 2005; Gertler & Karadi, 2015; Jarociński & Karadi, 2020).

6.3 Available Datasets and Replication Files

As the last section of this chapter, I have compiled a comprehensive list of important studies of the monetary policy shocks literature. I also indicate which software package, codes, original data, and other useful empirical work resources have been often made available by authors. I went back to year 1999 to review the literature and until the most recently published paper. My list is based on and extends the work of Ramey (2016) up to year 2023.

Table 6.3 reports the academic reference, DOI link, the adopted methodology, sample period, and all IT resources available online. My goal in framing the table is to provide doctoral students and young scholars with an overview of relevant published field papers and how to replicate those empirical findings. Most of the cited references included in the table are part of the previous chapter discussion.

References

Altavilla, C., Brugnolini, L., Gürkaynak, R. S., Motto, R., & Ragusa, G. (2019). Measuring Euro area monetary policy. *Journal of Monetary Economics, 108*(1), 162–179.

Barakchian, M. S., & Crowe, C. (2013). Monetary policy matters: Evidence from new shocks data. *Journal of Monetary Economics, 60*(8), 950–966.

Bauer, M. D., & Swanson, E. T. (2023). An alternative explanation for the "Fed Information Effect". *American Economic Review, 113*(3), 664–700.

Bernanke, B. S., Boivin, J., & Eliasz, P. (2005). Measuring the effects of Monetary Policy: A Factor-Augmented Vector Autoregressive (FAVAR) approach. *Quarterly Journal of Economics, 120*(1), 387–422.

[15] We do not report the code here, as it is analogous to that already presented, however, it is available upon request.

Cesa-Bianchi, A., Thwaites, G., & Vicondoa, A. (2020). Monetary policy transmission in the United Kingdom: A high frequency identification approach. *European Economic Review, 123*(1), 1–19.

Champagne, J., & Sekkel, R. (2018). Changes in monetary regimes and the identification of monetary policy shocks: Narrative evidence from Canada. *Journal of Monetary Economics, 99*(1), 72–87.

Christiano, L. J., Eichenbaum, M., & Evans, L. C. (1999). Monetary policy shocks: What have we learned and to what end? In *Handbook of macroeconomics* (Vol. 1 - Part A, pp. 65–148). Elsevier.

Cloyne, J., & Hürtgen, P. (2016). The macroeconomic effects of Monetary Policy: A new measure for the United Kingdom. *American Economic Journal: Macroeconomics, 8*(4), 75–102.

Coibion, O. (2012). Are the effects of Monetary Policy shocks big or small? *American Economic Journal: Macroeconomics, 4*(2), 1–32.

Faust, J., Swanson, E. T., & Wright, J. H. (2004). Identifying VARS based on high frequency futures data. *Journal of Monetary Economics, 51*(1), 1107–1131.

Gertler, M., & Karadi, P. (2015). Monetary policy surprises, credit costs, and economic activity. *American Economic Journal: Macroeconomics, 7*(1), 44–76.

Jarociński, M., & Karadi, P. (2020). Deconstructing Monetary Policy surprises—The role of information shocks. *American Economic Journal: Macroeconomics, 12*(2), 1–43.

Jordà, Ò. (2005). Estimation and inference of impulse responses by local projections. *American Economic Review, 95*(1), 161–182.

Kerssenfischer, M. (2022). Information effects of Euro area monetary policy. *Economics Letters, 216*(1), 1–6.

Kohler, T., & Cortina, J. M. (2019). Play it again, Sam! An analysis of constructive replication in the organizational sciences. *Journal of Management, 47*(2), 488–518.

Kuttner, K. N. (2001). Monetary policy surprises and interest rates: Evidence from the Fed funds futures market. *Journal of Monetary Economics, 47*(3), 523–544.

Luvsannyam, D., & Batmunkh, K. (2019). A factor-augmented vector autoregressive (FAVAR) approach for monetary policy: Replication of the empirical results in "measuring the effects of monetary policy". *Journal of Applied Econometrics, 34*(5), 820–821.

Miranda-Agrippino, S., & Ricco, G. (2021). The transmission of Monetary Policy shocks. *American Economic Journal: Macroeconomics, 13*(3), 74–107.

Murgia, L. M. (2020). The effect of monetary policy shocks on macroeconomic variables: Evidence from the Eurozone. *Economics Letters, 186*, 108803.

Pfaff, B. (2008). *Analysis of integrated and cointegrated time series with R* (2nd ed.). Springer.

Ramey, V. A. (2016). Macroeconomic shocks and their propagation. In *Handbook of macroeconomics* (pp. 71–162). Elsevier.

Romer, C., & Romer, D. H. (2004). A new measure of Monetary shocks: Derivation and implications. *American Economic Review, 94*(4), 1055–1084.

Romer, C. D., & Romer, D. H. (2023). Presidential address: Does Monetary Policy matter? The narrative approach after 35 years. *American Economic Review, 113*(6), 1395–1423.

Swanson, E. T. (2021). Measuring the effects of Federal Reserve forward guidance and asset purchases on financial markets. *Journal of Monetary Economics, 118*(1), 32–53.

Uhlig, H. (2005). What are the effects of monetary policy on output? Results from an agnostic identification procedure. *Journal of Monetary Economics, 52*(2), 389–419.

MIX
Papier aus verantwortungsvollen Quellen
Paper from responsible sources
FSC® C105338

If you have any concerns about our products,
you can contact us on
ProductSafety@springernature.com

In case Publisher is established outside the EU,
the EU authorized representative is:
Springer Nature Customer Service Center GmbH
Europaplatz 3, 69115 Heidelberg, Germany

Printed by Libri Plureos GmbH
in Hamburg, Germany